The S Murder Book

Sensational Scottish Murder Trials

Volume 1:
Perth, Angus and Fife

By the author of
Perthshire's Pound of Flesh and
Blood Beneath Ben Nevis

MARK BRIDGEMAN

TIPPERMUIR
· BOOKS LIMITED ·

The Scottish Murder Book – Volume 1 © 2024.
All rights reserved. The right of Mark Bridgeman to be
identified as the author of the Work has been asserted in
accordance with the Copyright, Designs & Patents Act 1988.

This first edition published and copyright 2024 by
Tippermuir Books Ltd, Perth, Scotland.

mail@tippermuirbooks.co.uk – www.tippermuirbooks.co.uk.

ISBN 978-1-913836-40-5 (paperback).

A CIP catalogue record for this book is available from
the British Library.

Project coordination and editorial by Paul S Philippou.

Cover design by Mark Bridgeman.

Editorial support: Steve Zajda.

Co-founders and publishers of Tippermuir Books:
Rob Hands, Matthew Mackie and Paul S Philippou.

Text design, layout, and artwork by Bernard Chandler [graffik].
Text set in Plantin Std Regular 10.2/13pt.

Printed and bound by Ashford Colour Press.

This book has been printed in the UK to
reduce transportation miles and their impact upon the
environment. It has been printed to comply with the
Forest Stewardship Council (FSC) Chain of Custody
requirements and paper sourcing from
responsibly managed sources.

The Scottish Murder Book

Sensational Scottish Murder Trials

Volume 1:
Perth, Angus and Fife

MARK BRIDGEMAN

TIPPERMUIR
· BOOKS LIMITED ·

ACKNOWLEDGEMENTS
AND REFERENCES

This book would not have been possible without the assistance of Paul S Philippou and the rest of the team at Tippermuir Books Ltd. Thank you for your support. I would also like to express my gratitude to Ellen McBride, Alexa Reid, AK Bell Libraries and everyone at Waterstones in Perth.

The following sources of information have also been invaluable in either helping to piece together the stories contained in this book, or for kindly supplying their permission for the reproduction of images and text:

Cinema Treasures, Scottish Enterprise, BBC Scotland, Canmore, Ordnance Survey, National Library of Scotland, Crime.Scot Legal Database. Perth Prison, Scotland's People, Findmypast, Ancestry UK, Scottish Law Society, British Newspaper Archive, newspapers.com, VLEX UK Case Law, CaseMine, University of Glasgow, University of Sheffield, British Execution Database, Scottish Indexes, National Records Scotland, capitalpunishment.org, Hansard Archives (House of Commons), Clyde Shipyards, Aberfeldy Museum and archive.org and the following newspapers, published resources and journals:

Crime, Prison and Punishment (1770 – 1935), The Police Code 1852, Caledonian Mercury, Fifeshire Advertiser, Fife Free Press, Edinburgh Evening News, The Scotsman, Perthshire Advertiser, Dundee Courier, Kirriemuir Observer, Lothian Life, The Trial of Margaret Tindall (John Smith Press, 1887), *The Omen of Dummie Ha's Wynd, Dead Man Talking* by Patricia Lucie, *Aberdeen Evening News, Aberdeen Free Press, Aberdeen Press and Journal, Berwick Advertiser, Dunfermline Journal, Edinburgh News, Glasgow Herald, Glasgow Evening News, Inverness Courier, Sunday Post, Sunday Mail, Daily Sketch, The Scottish Legal System* by Megan Dewart, *Scotland: History of a Nation* by David Ross and *Scottish Legal History* by The Stair Society.

ABOUT THE AUTHOR

After many years buried in research, Scottish-based writer Mark Bridgeman released his first book, *The River Runs Red*, in 2019. The book became an instant success and has been reprinted three times. Further best-selling titles, *Blood Beneath Ben Nevis* and *The Dark Side of the Dales* followed in 2020.

Mark's history of an abandoned Scottish community, *The Lost Village of Lawers*, achieved worldwide sales in 2021 when the village became a global news stories resulting in TV appearances on ITV and Channel 5.

In 2022, Mark was nominated for the John Bryne Writing Award as well as appearing on BBC Radio, Heartland FM, Vancouver Radio, BBC Alba and The History Channel.

The Nearly Man, Mark's biography of a little known Scottish war hero turned villain, has been nominated for the prestigious James Tait Black Biography Award and resulted in Mark being asked to guest speak at the prestigious Aberdeen Grammar School. His 2022 *Perthshire's Pound of Flesh* became Perth Waterstones' Book of the Year, voted for by their staff and customers.

Mark has also seen his stories serialised in newspaper form and adapted for Canadian radio. A member of the Federation of Scottish Writers and The Thomas Hardy Society, he has written for the academic *Thomas Hardy Journal* and contributes a popular series of blog articles for the West Highland Museum. In addition, he regularly appears at UK book festivals, presenting his unique sell-out event, 'Trial By Jury', and hosts regular talks at bookshops and local historical societies.

[*Blood Beneath Ben Nevis* and *Perthshire's Pound of Flesh* are available from www.tippermuirbooks.co.uk.]

THE SCOTTISH MURDER BOOK

CONTENTS

THE SCOTTISH MURDER BOOK

INTRODUCTION

'The law, in its majestic equality, forbids
the rich as well as the poor to sleep under bridges,
to beg in the streets, and to steal bread.'
Anatole France (French poet and journalist)

So hoped many of the prisoners hauled before the bench at the High Court in Perth during the past two centuries. Did the Scottish legal system really assure justice regardless of class and wealth or were some poor wretches condemned before their trials even began? There are fourteen fascinating, shocking and gruesome murders contained in this book which may prove or disprove the steadfastness of the Scottish legal system.

The murder of John Miller in his lonely tollhouse is just one of the many sensational and infamous Scottish murder trials held within a stone's throw of the River Tay, at the intimidating and sobering High Court at Perth. Was the man found guilty really Miller's murderer or did his killer escape justice?

Over the past two centuries, some of Scotland's most notorious and noteworthy murder cases from across Perthshire, Dundee, Angus and Fife have been tried in the Sheriffdom of Perth. In my previous book, *Perthshire's Pound of Flesh*, I examined a series of murderous crimes from the County of Perthshire, in which revenge appeared to be the overriding motive. In *The Perthshire Murder Book*, the importance of Perth as a centre of justice is examined, as we delve into fourteen of the most infamous trials to be held in the Fair City, including the exceedingly rare use of chloroform as a murder weapon, the killer who was released only to kill again, two possible miscarriages of justice, and a graphic description of the final moments of a murderer as they await the final drop.

In many of the cases featured here, you may find yourself

disagreeing vehemently with the jury's verdict. But, to sit as a juror in a murder trial – particularly in the era of the death penalty – is perhaps the ultimate responsibility.

When you have finished this collection, ask yourself honestly, what would your verdict have been – guilty or not guilty?

Mark Bridgeman
markbridgemanauthor.co.uk

1 – THE BOTTLE AND THE BREAD KNIFE

June 1968 – The first five and ten pence coins have recently been introduced into the economy, in the run up to decimalisation, the *Abortion Act* became law and the National Health Service reintroduced prescription charges.

Temperatures had been well above average in Scotland during the first half of the month. Perth was bathed in glorious sunshine on the morning of Wednesday, 19 June, as a shabbily dressed young man, with cuts on his face and hands, was observed by several motorists as he walked slowly out of the Fair City, along the grass verge of the Glasgow Road. Occasionally, he raised his thumb, in a vain attempt to secure a lift. However, the unkempt appearance of this particular hitchhiker meant it would be more than an hour until a passing Hillman Hunter finally slowed down and pulled over.

'Need a lift?' the driver enquired.

'Aye,' came the young man's reply.

'Whereabouts you heading for?'

'Dover.'

'Hop in, I can take you a bit of the way.'

Despite the hitchhiker's dishevelled appearance, the obliging driver leaned across and opened the passenger door for his dishevelled travelling companion, and the car soon sped away from the city. Little did the driver realise, this hitchhiker would soon be the subject of a massive police manhunt.

Meanwhile, Perth Police had been summoned to George Summer's home, known as 'New Land', in Tulloch Road, close to the Dorran Construction Works. Dorran produced, on average, ten new prefabricated homes a week from their Perth factory, shipping them around the country. George Summers was a costing clerk for the company and 'New Land' was a 'tied property', a two-story semi-detached house belonging to the company.

1

When officers arrived at the house on Wednesday afternoon, they found the badly injured body of 26-year-old George slumped on the floor of his living room. His face and clothes were saturated in blood and the rug beneath him stained a crimson red. An ambulance was called but sadly Summers passed away from severe blood loss shortly afterwards. His death quickly became a murder enquiry. Detective Chief Inspector Alex King, head of Perth and Kinross CID, acted decisively and issued a statement at a hastily arranged press conference: 'There are obvious signs of a struggle in the house. Mr Summer had suffered severe injuries and had clearly fought for his life. I can confirm the police are treating this matter as one of murder. We are appealing to the public for any information about Mr Summer's movements on Tuesday night.'

Having already been informed of several sightings of an unkempt individual attempting to hitchhike out of Perth, DCI King added, 'We are also anxious to contact any driver who picked up a young, scruffily dressed man, with two cuts on his face, thumbing a lift away from Perth early on Wednesday, particularly on the main Glasgow Road. In addition, we understand that the victim, Mr Summers, had recently become estranged from his wife and two small children. Although, whether these incidents are connected, we cannot say at this stage.'

'Can you say what injuries the victim suffered?' asked one reporter.

'I cannot say at this moment,' answered DCI King, 'Our enquiries are ongoing at this stage.'

With a suspect on the loose, DCI King did not wish to alarm the public by revealing that the victim had suffered multiple wounds from what appeared to be a broken bottle and a breadknife.

Although the sketch of the suspect that the police wished to question was a sparse one, it would not be long until officers received a break on the case when the driver of a beige Hillman Hunter came forward. He remembered picking up a hitchhiker early that morning. The witness was able to confirm that his passenger was intending to travel 600 miles to Dover and had chatted about catching a ferry to the Continent. Police and port officials in Dover were notified and it was only a matter of hours until a young man fitting that description was spotted, attempting to board a ferry bound for France. He was detained while DCI King and another officer flew south from Turnhouse Airport in Edinburgh to interview him.

The young man transpired to be a seventeen-year-old from Perth by the name of William Ebenezer Robertson. Robertson who, at the time of his arrest, was wearing a cardigan and coat belonging to the victim, and had several marks on his face, claimed that he had met George Summers on Tuesday evening but knew nothing about his death.

Once back in Perth, the decision was made to charge Robertson. The following morning he was transported from Perth Police Station to a basement cell at the High Court in Tay Street. Once inside, he was ushered upstairs, with a raincoat draped over his head to disguise his appearance from the waiting reporters. Robertson was then escorted along the corridor to Sheriff Prain's anteroom where the raincoat was removed. Standing in a blue suit and open-necked shirt, Robertson was then formally charged: 'William Ebenezer Robertson, of no fixed abode, the charge is that on June 18th or 19th, in the house known as New Land, Tulloch Road, Perth, occupied by George Goodson Summers, you did assault Mr Summers by striking him numerous blows on the face and body, with a broken bottle or similar instrument and stabbed him in the neck with a knife and murdered him. Do you wish to enter a plea?'

Robertson stood in stony silence as a trial date was set for Tuesday, 1 October 1968 at the High Court in Perth. No formal plea was entered and he was led away under escort.

In what might seem a strange quirk of the Scottish legal system, Robertson was also charged with 'Stealing a coat, cardigan, clock, diary, and radio' from the victim. If the charge of murder failed, at least the Crown had this lesser charge to fall back on, although this was clearly little comfort for Mr Summers' estranged wife and children.

William Robertson's appointed defence advocate, the flamboyant Lionel Daiches QC, now had three months to prepare an adequate defence, despite the strong circumstantial evidence against his client, which included being in possession of the victim's clothes, marks from a fight on his face, and admitting to meeting with Mr Summers on the night of his death. Nevertheless, Robertson's troubled background provided Lionel Daiches with adequate grounds. Robertson, at the time of the offence, was of no fixed abode, possessed a juvenile record, was unemployed, appeared to suffer from mental health challenges – possibly linked to alcohol dependency – and had spent many nights sleeping rough or what might now be called 'sofa surfing'. Fortunately, thanks to the introduction of the Legal Aid and Advice Act 1949, William Robertson was entitled to a defence advocate of Mr Daiches' experience. A luxury which might not have been available a generation earlier.

Prior to the trial, Daiches lodged a special defence of 'Not guilty on the grounds of insanity at the time of the offence and was therefore not responsible for his actions.' Robertson also denied striking Mr Summers with a weapon or with his fists and to stealing any items from the victim's home.

Robertson's trial opened on 1 October with Lord Stott presiding. After hearing the defendant's newly worded and revised plea of insanity, the case for the Crown was then outlined by the Advocate-Depute for Perthshire: 'George Summers and William Robertson had met, purely by chance, at the Ace of Clubs public house in Perth on Tuesday 18th June. At that time, the victim, Mr Summers, was lonely and drowning his sorrows, following the recent break-up of his marriage. His wife had moved out, taking their two young children with her. Robertson and Mr Summers got talking and Mr Summers, anxious for some company, invited the young man back to his home to eat a takeaway. Robertson agreed, and the two men left the public house and returned to Tulloch Road.'

This is the statement given to the police by William Robertson following his arrest: 'An argument then started, when Mr Summers accused me of stealing some money. Summers attacked me and I killed him in self-defence.' Mr Robertson then added the following words to his statement: 'I admits to causing Summers' death by punching him, hitting him with a bottle and stabbing him.' However, Mr Robertson now claims that he was insane at the time of the murder.'

In view of the amended testimony from William Robertson, in which he admitted killing Mr Summers, Lord Stott ordered that the trial would now be restricted to medical evidence alone. It would now be the responsibility of the jury to decide if the accused man was guilty of murder, or not responsible for his actions at the time of the offence.

Professor Gilbert Forbes of Glasgow University presented the forensic evidence on behalf of the Crown: 'Your honour, I examined both the victim's body and the injuries on the defendant. The deceased had died as a result of severe blood loss and trauma. He was found with a breadknife sticking from the neck. The knife had entered the victim's neck in a downward motion, with such force that more than seven inches of the blade were in the body. The deceased had sustained many other injuries in what, in my opinion, was a violent, vicious, and determined attack.'

'Thank you, Professor, and did you also examine the defendant's injuries?'

'Yes. At the time of his arrest, the defendant had a quarter inch cut on one hand and two small scars on one side of his face – trifling injuries in comparison with the deceased man.'

Next, came the expert medical evidence from two consultant psychiatrists employed by the Crown to examine William Robertson during his time on remand in Perth Prison.

Dr Thomas Wylie, who had interviewed Robertson on a number of occasions over the preceding months, expressed the view that the accused man, 'Despite his young years was responsible for his actions at that time.' This was endorsed by Dr Smith, who said, 'In my opinion the defendant is sane and fit to plead.'

Speaking for the defence, Lionel Daiches QC countered by explaining, 'The savagery of the attack on Mr Summers, the defendant's subsequent behaviour, and other circumstances can surely *only* lead to the conclusion that my client was mentally ill at the time. I now call to the stand on behalf of the defence, two eminent doctors in the field of psychiatry, Dr Aitken and Dr Gordon, who have spoken to Mr Robertson at depth.'

Firstly, Dr Robert Aitken from Edinburgh University's Department of Psychiatry, concluded that 'Various factors, including Robertson's previous anti-social behaviour and juvenile history, contributed to the view that he was suffering from mental illness at the time of the offence.'

Dr Gordon testified that Robertson was, 'in my opinion, technically sane at the time of the crime', but recommended that he should be 'commissioned to a State mental hospital.'

So, with medical opinion on William Robertson's mental state divided, Lord Stott summed up the case for the jury of eight men and seven women: 'Members of the jury, the statement lodged by the defendant in which he admitted assaulting, striking and stabbing him, and that Mr Summers died as the consequence of the injuries inflicted by him, does not necessarily mean that the accused is guilty of the charge of murder, or that he was insane. These are matters for you to determine now that you have heard all the evidence in this case. Four consultant psychiatrists are divided in their opinion of Robertson's sanity and his fitness to plead. Two said he was sane at the time of the offence. Another said he was technically sane, but recommended his commission to the State mental hospital. The fourth said he was insane. It is now your task to reflect on all the evidence presented here. Please now retire and consider your verdict.'

And with that, the jury duly retired while William Robertson was led back to his cell to nervously await the decision of the fifteen jurors. His advocate advised him that:

'The longer the jury take in their deliberations, the more the likelihood of a favourable verdict. The less time they take, the less likely the verdict will be in our favour.'

Lionel Daiches proved to be correct – but it was not the verdict his client had hoped for. After just eighteen minutes the jury returned with a unanimous rejection of Robertson's insanity plea. He was found 'guilty', both of murder and of the lesser charge of theft. Lord Stott, perhaps with a sense of regret in his voice – then addressed the prisoner: 'William Ebenezer Robertson. You have been found guilty on a charge of murder and theft. There is only one sentence I can pass. You are sentenced to be detained at Her Majesty's pleasure.'

Despite his tender years and the divide in the expert medical testimony, Robertson was not given the benefit of the doubt. No appeal was launched and the seventeen-year-old was incarcerated at Polmont Young Offenders Institution. Whether he received any psychiatric help during his stay there is not known. However, because he was found to be sane at the time of Mr Summers' murder, it does not seem likely.

One question remains. Was the defence team's strategy at trial the correct one? A plea of insanity was undoubtedly a gamble, since it suggests little remorse or contrition on the part of a defendant, should they subsequently be found sane at the time of their offence. It also offers the presiding judge little leeway in sentencing. A 'guilty' verdict, following a plea of 'not guilty on the grounds of insanity', suggests both an attempt to avoid prison on a legal technicality, and a failure on the part of the guilty person to accept responsibility for their crime.

Perhaps a better tactic for the defence might have been to place an element of doubt in the jury's mind. It is an intrinsic principle of any murder trial that the accused person is innocent until proven guilty beyond reasonable doubt. Although it is not the responsibility of the defence to suggest that other suspects may have committed the crime, a tactic of hinting at that possibility frequently has the effect of planting an element of doubt into a juror's mind. In the case of Mr Summers, at the time of his death in 1968, he had recently separated from his wife, Sarah, who had in turn begun a relationship with another man.

It later transpired that, following a series of violent arguments between the pair, Sarah Summers was arrested in 1974 and charged with attempted murder, after stabbing her new partner in the chest with a kitchen knife. The charge was later reduced to one of assault and Mrs Summers was placed on probation for three years, with the added condition that she undergo psychiatric treatment at the discretion of a court appointed doctor.

Sarah Summers' new partner presumably forgave her, as she informed the court that they still intended to marry after he had recovered! It was a promise she kept. The couple remained married until her death in 2013.

Had the defence in William Robertson's trial introduced even the slightest possibility that someone else had harboured a motive to kill George Summers, perhaps the jury might have been persuaded that an element of doubt existed in the case, and may have returned a verdict of 'not proven', or even 'not guilty'. Sometimes the verdict of a jury can depend, as much on the strategies employed by the opposing advocates, as on the evidence presented. On such tiny margins justice is often decided.

2 – MANHUNT FOR A MURDERER
(Part One)

Friday, 19 February 1909 – At precisely 11am, just like clock-work, Michael Brown, a fifteen-year-old apprentice clerk at G & J Johnston, left the firm's weaving mill in East Wemyss, on the Fife coast, to catch the morning tramcar to the nearby town of Buckhaven. Once there, his weekly duty was to collect the company's wages from the Royal Bank of Scotland then return to East Wemyss by lunchtime, in order that the millworkers' pay-packets could be made up. Although only fifteen, Michael was a popular and honest lad who was trusted to safely collect the employees' weekly payroll of £85, largely in coins, for its short journey back to the mill. However, the sum – equivalent to around £13,000 today – was a not insignificant one and the bulky bag required to carry it, together with his predictable routine, had unknowingly attracted unwanted attention.

Michael Brown arrived at the Buckhaven branch of the Royal Bank of Scotland around 11.15am on that Friday morning. Alexander Lawson, the bank clerk, cashed the G & J Johnston cheque given to him by Brown and began to count out the £85 requested by the company – £25 in £1 notes, £20 in half-sovereigns and £40 in silver. Once the money had been placed inside his leather Gladstone bag, Brown left the bank and walked to the Muiredge Stopping Station on Wemyss & District Tramways line.

It was now 11.30am. A miner named Henry Saunders, who had just finished his shift, was standing on the street corner opposite the bank engaged in conversation with another man. The other man, 23-year-old Alexander Edmonstone, had previously worked as a miner, but was now unemployed. He had also worked as a carter at G & J Johnston, and undoubtedly knew and recognised Michael Brown, who had been employed at the firm for the past eighteen months.

stable Alexander Stewart lived nearby, and was
noned. By the time he arrived at the scene,
wn was already dead. Although the constable
oung boy well, his body was so disfigured and
swo.   nd his face so caked with blood that it took the
constable a moment to recognise him. Stewart then contacted
Sergeant Robert Clydesdale and the two men began to
question passers-by on School Wynd and High Road.

Before long, several witnesses were able to confirm that
they had seen Alexander Edmonstone leaving the tramcar at
the same time as Michael Brown. In fact, Edmonstone had
made little effort to conceal the fact. A group of miners
standing at the top of School Wynd had even exchanged
greetings with him. Meanwhile, Edmonstone appeared to
have vanished, and he quickly became the prime suspect. Just
before 4pm, police officers Stewart and Clydesdale visited
Edmonstone's parents' home in Main Street. However,
according to his father Walter Edmonstone, their son had left
home around 10.30am that morning and had not returned.
Sergeant Clydesdale then asked Edmonstone's mother for a
photograph of her son, but when she returned, it seemed that
Alexander Edmonstone had already destroyed all the family's
photographs in which he appeared, as well as removing all his
clothing from the closet. It was an ominous and chilling sign.

Meanwhile, a quarter of a mile away, a miner named
Thomas Moodie was walking close to the shore, among the
ruins of MacDuff's Castle, when he chanced upon the empty
discarded Gladstone bag, together with a torn envelope, and
a Royal Bank of Scotland bankbook. It appeared that
Edmonstone had made his way in a south-easterly direction
from School Wynd, through the wood, along the course of the
burn, before ascending the bank behind the brewery.
Unobserved, he had then divided the heavy contents of the
leather money bag equally between the pockets of his coat,
before discarding the items in the overgrown gorse bushes
between the caves and the ruins of MacDuff's Castle. He may

not have expected the money bag to contain so many coins (£40's worth), which would have, undoubtedly, both weighed him down and appeared conspicuous in the extreme.

Alexander Edmonstone was next witnessed hurrying past Newton Farm, keeping close to the line of the trees. Nonetheless, he was assumed to be just a poacher seeking to evade the gamekeeper. He walked along the Kirkcaldy High Road before stopping at one of the Julian Cottages (the miners' houses at Earlseat Colliery) to ask for a glass of water and a brush to clean his clothes. When the elderly householder, Mr Hardie, appeared uninclined to help him, Edmonstone made his excuses and hurried away. A dog barked loudly at him as he turned to leave, bringing unwanted attention to the fugitive, and he moved briskly away. The elderly Mr Hardie later remarked, 'He was walking fast, although evidently not wishing to attract attention. He was wearing a brownish suit, his cap pulled down well over his eyes. There was no sign of blood on his clothing, but his trousers were covered in mud, and his clothes had whitewash on them.'

Within a matter of hours, a full-scale manhunt was launched for the suspected killer. Major Edwin Richardson's famous bloodhounds were transported from London to East Wemyss especially, on a privately chartered overnight train. The dogs, Solferino and Waterloo, were already celebrities in their own right and their presence in the chase created almost as much public interest as the quest for the murderer.

Finally, at first light on Saturday, 20 February, now more than eighteen hours since Michael Brown's murder, the manhunt could begin. After being given the scent from the leather money bag and a pillow taken from Alexander Edmonstone's bed, the bloodhounds were unleashed across the hard, frosty ground in pursuit of the fugitive. A 'dragging line' of police officers, led by Sergeant Cummings from Cupar, accompanied the dogs as they picked up the killer's trail across fields and lanes, as he headed rapidly in a north-westerly direction from East Wemyss, apparently avoiding the population centres of Glenrothes and Freuchie. The hounds proved to be on the right track when they discovered that Edmonstone had stopped at a remote farmhouse where he had requested a glass of water. Unfortunately, the authorities were now almost a day behind their man, but they took some comfort, as the hounds at least appeared to be on the right trail.

Meanwhile, approximately fifteen hours earlier, darkness was descending. Edmonstone was now north of Glenrothes, having avoided being spotted by the population of that busy town. He walked purposefully north along the main road (now the A92) before branching left at Muirhead and heading towards Falkland.

A day later, somewhere near that junction, the bloodhounds lost the fugitive's scent. Conceivably, Edmonstone had retraced his steps to mislead the dogs, Major Richardson surmised, or perhaps waded through one of the many small burns that flow from the Lomond Hills, or even hitched a ride from an unsuspecting farmer or passing horse and cart. Whatever the reason, Major Richardson was forced to give up the chase and return to England. The dogs had been partially successful, nevertheless, and it was now, at least, known in which direction Edmonstone had been heading on the previous evening. Major Richardson, already the country's leading dog trainer would later establish the British Army's War Dog Training School and serve with distinction in the Great War.

Returning to the events of the previous day, it was now late on Friday afternoon. With the Lomond Hills to his left and the open farm fields to his right, Edmonstone quickly covered the three miles to Falkland. He stopped at a small shop in the town to purchase some biscuits, before heading north-west towards Strathmiglo. The police, still at least fifteen hours behind and not knowing in which direction their quarry had headed, now relied on information from the public. Fortunately for the police (although they would not receive this information until Saturday morning), and no doubt emboldened by his success so far, Edmonstone had called at George Knox's draper's shop in Strathmiglo late on Friday afternoon, and purchased a new suit, an overcoat, a muffler, and a cap – paying for his purchase with three half-sovereigns, three crowns, and two half-crown pieces – money stolen from Michael Brown.

The draper, curious at the scruffily dressed customer bursting into his shop as he was about to close, enquired politely why might anyone need a completely new outfit in such a hurry. Edmonstone replied, 'I have been at Falkland visiting my aunt, and I am now returning to Perth to see my mother. It is ten years since I have seen her, I ran away from home. Now that I am returning I wish to be as respectably dressed as possible.'

Edmonstone donned his new overcoat and cap, and with his new suit wrapped in a brown paper parcel, headed along Strathmiglo's High Street to the railway station. Once there, he purchased a single ticket to Perth, via Mawcarse Junction, on the Fife and Kinross Line, then boarded the 6.19pm Friday evening train. At Mawcarse Junction, perhaps feeling more comfortable now that he had successfully placed some distance between himself and the scene of his crime, the fugitive even coolly asked the stationmaster, 'Which platform for Perth?'

'Cross to the other side, sir', the stationmaster answered, as he watched Edmonstone with his bundle under his arm, cross to the other platform and board the 6.38pm connection to Perth.

Edmonstone emerged unseen at Perth General Railway Station, now 30 miles away from the scene of his crime, and walked the short distance to the Salutation Temperance Hotel in South Street. He spent a quiet night there among the other unsuspecting hotel guests, before changing into his new attire and discarding some of his old, soiled and travel-stained clothing (on which the pockets were still misshapen by the weight of the stolen coins).

The following morning (Saturday, 20 February), as Major Richardson and his bloodhounds were just beginning the hunt for their prey in Fife, Alexander Edmonstone was witnessed returning to Perth Railway Station, where he purchased a third-class single ticket to Edinburgh. He boarded the 9.55am service to the capital. Fortunately, the wanted man's description had already been circulated to police and railway stations and, when a man bearing a strong likeness to the fugitive was seen boarding the Edinburgh train at Perth, a message was urgently cabled to detectives in Edinburgh who placed three burly plain-clothed detectives at both Waverley and Haymarket Stations. Nevertheless, despite the presence of these officers – who made what they would later describe as 'a thorough search' of the platform and carriages – no one matching Edmonstone's appearance alighted at either station. It was surmised that he had either disembarked from the train at an earlier station, or conceivably even jumped from the carriage door at a slow point or signal stop during the journey (a possibility, strangely and coincidentally, reminiscent of Perth-born John Buchan's famous creation Richard Hannay during his escape across Scotland in the 1935 film *The Thirty-Nine Steps*). The trail for the wanted man had now gone cold. The fugitive had slipped the net.

To make matters worse, on the following day, it would emerge that Alexander Edmonstone's ticket had actually been surrendered at Haymarket Station, meaning the wanted man had either nonchalantly walked straight past the waiting detectives on the platform, or had swapped tickets with another passenger on the journey and then alighted elsewhere. Edmonstone, who by now might conceivably be travelling to any station in the country, was clearly a brazen and resourceful criminal. Detectives, it seems, were clearly playing catch-up. It was now time to raise the stakes, as the manhunt soon became a national one.

With Edmonstone now possibly anywhere in the country, or perhaps even attempting to flee abroad, a close watch was placed at ports across the country. Leith Police received a reported sighting of their suspect at Leith docks, however, the report proved to be the first of many red herrings in the manhunt.

A substantial reward of £100 (£15,000 today) was offered and a full description of the wanted man was issued:

'WANTED – £100 REWARD for

MURDER AND ROBBERY

Alexander Edmonstone, 23 years of age, Miner or Carter, 5 feet 9 inches or thereby in height, slender build, auburn or reddish-brown hair, dark eyes, full ruddy face, hitherto clean shaved, wanting three teeth in front of upper jaw, A. E. stop tattooed on right forearm, Scotch accent. Native of Edinburgh. Edmonstone purchased the following new clothing: Mottled yellow brown tweed jacket suit, dark grey showerproof coat, single-breasted with turned-over cuffs. Black bone Buttons, sleeve lining, black, blue, and white stripes. Dark grey single peaked cap. Size 7 or 7¾. "The Dunkeld" stamped in black on the inside yellow lining. May continue to shave, or may not. May acquire artificial teeth, may dye his hair, or may otherwise alter his appearance. Will probably endeavour to leave the country. The above reward will be paid by the subscriber to any person furnishing such information as shall lead to the apprehension and conviction of the person or persons who committed said crime.

J TENNANT GORDON – Chief Constable of Fife.'

Meanwhile, Edmonstone, after having successfully evaded the Edinburgh Police, boarded a Dunfermline bound train at Waverley Station. Once again, he proved to be one step ahead of the authorities by alighting at Dunfermline and purchasing another single ticket to Glasgow Queen Street, which first required returning to Haymarket Station in Edinburgh. A route the police would hardly be likely to consider. Nevertheless, Edmonstone was remembered by a porter at Dunfermline Lower Station when he appeared most anxious to read the headlines in the porter's newspaper.

As is often the case in such circumstances, the offering of a substantial reward was accompanied by as many false leads as useful ones. On Tuesday, 22 February, Glasgow detectives visited a large sandstone boarding house in Renfrew Street, where a man matching Edmonstone's description had registered. Fortunately for the fugitive, he had informed the landlady that he was 'going out to meet a pal at Buchanan Street Station,' and that he 'would be back later.' However, by the time officers arrived Edmonstone had already departed, leaving behind some old undergarments. Although a plain-clothed detective remained on watch outside the property, the fugitive never returned.

Perhaps Edmonstone had planned to return to the boarding house but became suspicious when he spotted someone loitering outside, or possibly, it was yet another carefully planned decoy in his clearly well thought out escape plan.

Detectives now believed that the fugitive was attempting to leave Glasgow, either by ship, or by train, perhaps to lose himself among the bustling populations in one of the great metropolises of England.

A careful watch was maintained at railway stations and at ports along the west coast of Scotland and England. In the meantime, detectives followed a number of other leads in the hunt for Michael Brown's killer. Firstly, a Stirlingshire miner thought he had seen a man matching Edmonstone's description, counting gold coins, on an Edinburgh to Glasgow train. However, the lead turned out to be false. A more promising tip came from Edinburgh when 'a suspicious and shifty looking man' pawned a watch and chain in a Canongate pawnbrokers. The same man then changed several Royal Bank of Scotland £1 notes. However, upon checking, the banknotes did not seem to correspond to those given to Michael Brown at the Buckhaven branch, and the watch and chain did not match the items stolen from the murdered boy. Nevertheless, detectives did not rule out the possibility that Edmonstone had deliberately staged the incident to convince detectives that he had remained in the capital city. This theory was strengthened when it was discovered that the wanted man's family originated from Edinburgh, and that Edmonstone had worked there as a boy. Perhaps he had paid an accomplice to plant his old clothing in the Renfrew Street boarding house in Glasgow, to throw the police off the scent, when he had in fact remained in Edinburgh. Detectives were ordered to consider all possibilities. Neither lead, however, provided any new information for the under pressure police.

Meanwhile, on Monday, 22 February, a memorial service was held for Michael Brown at the United Free Church in East Wemyss. The Reverend George Low described the murdered boy as, 'a gentle and guileless boy, diligent in his business and dutiful in his home – a good son and good brother. An evil beast hath devoured him.' As many as 5,000 people lined the streets of East Wemyss, and local dignitaries including the Member of Parliament for West Fife, Mr John Hope, packed the cemetery grounds as Michael was buried, just two months shy of his sixteenth birthday.

3 – MANHUNT FOR A MURDERER
(Part Two)

March 1909 – As February became March, two arrests were made, one in Glasgow and one in Dumbarton. Both men vigorously denied being the wanted fugitive. The suspect arrested in Glasgow was quickly released when examined, as he proved to have no tattoo and to be in possession of a fine set of teeth! However, the young man arrested in Dumbarton proved to be such a good likeness it took several hours before detectives were convinced, and finally agreed to release him.

The first confirmed sighting of Alexander Edmonstone came on Wednesday, 24 February, this time to the west of Glasgow. A railway signalman on his way to work noticed a man coming out of a wooden shed on the edge of the Ardmore estate, between Cardross and Helensburgh. It was 6am, and the man had clearly spent a cold and uncomfortable night sheltering in the shed. The Cardross Police were informed; although, by the time officers reached the location, Edmonstone had vanished. The same man was spotted again later that same day in woods off the Glenoran Road, at the west end of Craigendoran, on the outskirts of Helensburgh, and identified by witnesses (who had all been shown an image of Edmonstone) as definitely being the person in the photograph. A large dragnet was thrown around the wood and police, assisted by local gamekeepers, surrounded the area. It was decided to wait until daylight to enter the woods, lest their quarry escape under cover of darkness. At dawn, the officers finally moved in. Nevertheless, despite a thorough search the prey once again managed to elude the hunters.

Meanwhile, constabularies in other parts of the country were not idle. As far south as Liverpool a detective, who knew Edmonstone by sight, was stationed at the docks and given the task of scrutinising every passenger bound for Canada on

RMS *Dominion* and *Hesperian*, or heading for South America aboard the SS *Oronsa*. The detective remained in Liverpool for seven days, ultimately expanding his search to include any long-distance steamers heading for the colonies. The efforts were eventually abandoned when no one matching Edmonstone's description was seen boarding any vessel leaving the docks.

All information regarding any potential sightings of Edmonstone was coordinated through the headquarters of Fife Constabulary at Cupar. Conversely, however, as the number of officers employed in the search for the fugitive increased, the number of confirmed sightings grew less. A number of Fifeshire miners and police officers, all who knew Edmonstone personally were placed at the disposal of Glasgow Police, should the missing man be spotted on the streets of the city.

With the exception of two possible sightings, one in Dundee, and one in Larkhall, South Lanarkshire – neither of which could be confirmed – it seemed that the wanted man had successfully escaped. It was even rumoured that he may have been en route for the colonies, where he was known to have associates.

It would be more than a month after the murder of Michael Brown that the fugitive from justice would finally be captured; not in Glasgow, nor Fife, but 260 miles away in Manchester.

At teatime on Thursday, 25 March 1909 at a small but respectable Victorian lodging house, 16 Brunswick Street in the centre of Manchester, a young motor car driver by the name of Albert Edwards came down the stairs from his room and was surprised to see three smartly dressed men standing in the lobby. He passed them with a casual nod, as he walked along the narrow passage, to take his place at the kitchen tea table. He called out for his food, but the landlady, Mrs Bridgeworth, did not appear at the door as was the custom. Instead, the three men who had been standing in the hallway entered. The first man introduced himself:

'I am Detective-Inspector Riding from Manchester Constabulary, this is Detective-Sergeant Allen, and Detective Idson. Who are you, and what is your name?'

The young man replied without hesitation, 'I'm Albert Edwards, I am a motor car driver.'

'Are you not Alexander Edmonstone, the man wanted for the murder of the boy Michael Brown at East Wemyss, in Fifeshire?'

The cornered man hesitated momentarily, as if taking stock, before answering, 'Yes, I am the man you want.'

He was arrested and a telegram was wired .to Fife Constabulary. The Chief Constable, James Tennant Gordon, who was attending a meeting of the Provincial Grand Masonic Lodge in Kinghorn at that moment, was sent for. He quickly dispatched two officers to Manchester, to identify and return with Edmonstone.

It would transpire that the offer of a reward for Edmonstone's arrest had directly led to his discovery. John Atherton, a fellow lodger at 16 Brunswick Street, had noticed a wanted poster for Edmonstone at the Whitworth Street Police Station in the city. He had been struck by the strong resemblance of the wanted man to his new neighbour in the lodging house. However, rather than jumping to conclusions, John Atherton devised a cunning test to decide once-and-for-all if Albert Edwards was in fact Alexander Edmonstone. When Atherton returned to the lodging house, he engaged the man calling himself 'Albert Edwards' in casual conversation, during which he asked, 'Albert, what is the time?'

Atherton observed the watch and chain intently, as 'Albert Edwards' produced them from his pocket. They matched the description of Michael Brown's watch and chain perfectly.

Even then, Atherton did nothing to arouse Edmonstone's suspicions. He sent the landlady, Mrs Bridgeworth, to view the wanted poster for herself before the pair then decided to contact the police. The detectives were initially sceptical, until Mrs Bridgeworth described her lodger in more detail.

Edmonstone had first called at 16 Brunswick Street approximately a week after the murder (on Friday, 26 February). He had knocked on the door and explained to the landlady, 'I am a motor car driver, and I'm looking for lodgings.

I've been working at the Belle Vue Motor Show and they put me in digs above a restaurant in London Road, but I'd prefer to find some private lodgings.'

According to Mrs Bridgeworth he brandished a motor car driver's licence in the name of Albert Edwards, before adding, 'I've secured a job at a garage in Deansgate.'

'He was a quiet, well-behaved lodger,' she explained to the police, 'he kept regular hours, and went to his work every morning. It was his custom at dinnertime to go upstairs to wash the dirt off his hands.'

She continued her explanation to the police, 'When in conversation with him, the talk often turned to Scotland. I told him that I prefer to stay here, as I felt safer. He told me, "A poor lad has been killed there, and they cannot get the murderer." Yes, that was a cruel job.'

Following his arrest a search was made of Edmonstone's room, in which detectives uncovered a Gladstone bag containing £42 15 shillings (not the bag stolen from Michael Brown), and a homemade improvised cudgel; this suggested that perhaps Edmonstone had another murderous robbery planned. It was not immediately clear from where Edmonstone had managed to obtain a motor car driving license in the name of 'Albert Edwards.' It was either a piece of extraordinary luck on Edmonstone's part, to have located a victim with the same initials; however, it is more probable that he either stole a blank licence or obtained a forgery. In 1909, driving licences were a comparatively new and primitive affair, having only been introduced six years earlier following the passing of the Motor Car Act 1903. The holder's details were handwritten and easily forged. This provided Edmonstone, should he be asked, with a convenient way of explaining the 'A.E.' tattoo on his right forearm.

Two hundred people gathered outside the County Buildings in Cupar as an exhausted, and handcuffed, Edmonstone was dragged inside, following his overnight train journey from England. He was charged by Sheriff Armour as follows:

'That you did, in a public water-closet in School Wynd, East Wemyss village, rob Michael Swinton Brown, clerk, of a bag containing £85 of money and of a watch and chain; and that you did assault him, and did seize him by the throat and press it with your hands and a handkerchief, and did kick him on the head, or knock his head against a hard object, or strike him on the head with a blunt instrument, fracturing his skull, and did thus murder him.'

Edmonstone answered in quaking tone, 'I have nothing to say.' He was then removed, past the booing crowd, and remanded at Perth Prison.

The trial date was set for Tuesday, 8 June at the High Court in Perth. Lord Guthrie would preside and Edmonstone's solicitor, David Carswell, appointed J A Christie KC to defend his client.

With his trial looming, the accused man was permitted to write one letter to his mother, who had been anxiously awaiting news of her son. The letter was written on the prison's blue paper and carried the official 'Approved' stamp of the Governor:

'No. 447,094 Edmonstone, HM Prison Perth 29/3/09

My dear Mother, Just a few lines to let you know that I am still thinking about all of you. How are you all keeping? I hope that father is still keeping up, and you too, mother. How is Little Willie keeping? Robert, Tommy, and Sophia? Tell them I was asking for them, and tell them to keep up their spirits for my sake. My dearest mother, I don't know what you will think of me, but try to think the best, for this black cloud which is falling on my head is also falling on yours. I would like to see some of you if you can manage it or care to come and see me. Father and mother, try and come up see me. I am a bit afraid to ask you, but I hope you will always call me your son yet, and think of me, for I am always thinking of you all day and night. You are never out of my mind, dearest mother.

I pray daily for you, for I have broken all your hearts, and I hope you do the same for me, dear mother. I think I'll close, I feel I am going to break down. Give my best love to all. Hope this will find you all well, as it leaves me.

Write and let me know when you can come to see me. Best love. From your affectionate son, Alex.'

The day of Edmonstone's trial finally arrived. A large crowd gathered on Tay Street and the officers escorting the prisoner the short distance from Perth Prison were forced to enter via a side door on South Street. When the doors of the main courtroom were opened a throng of 'Perth rowdies, Fifeshire miners, and hysterical elderly ladies' (as they were described in the *Perthshire Advertiser*) burst through, all keen to find the most advantageous viewing point in the public gallery.

Following a fanfare of trumpets and an opening prayer by the Reverend Lee, Edmonstone entered a plea of 'not guilty.' His advocate, J A Christie KC, also confirmed to the court that his client was entering a special plea, 'That at the time of the act, he was insane, and therefore not responsible for his actions.'

Mr A M Anderson KC, the Advocate-Depute, opened the case for the prosecution with a vivid description of the tragic events. The first witness, Michael Brown's employer Mr James Johnston, then explained that:

'Michael Brown, who was our junior clerk, had been in the habit of going to the bank in Buckhaven to collect the wages. He had done so since October 1907, and was always instructed to take the tramcar both ways. He was bright and trustworthy. It was quite well known in Wemyss that Brown went to Buckhaven to collect the wages.'

'And would the accused man have been aware of this fact?'

'Well, he had done some carting work at the factory before.'

The next witness, William Johnston, described being asked by the police to identify the deceased: 'At first, I could not identify him, either from his features or his clothing, the first being so disfigured, and the latter so dirty. However, I did conclude that the body was that of Michael Brown from a post office label bearing his handwriting and a piece of pencil in his pocket.'

Henry Saunders from Buckhaven testified next: 'I had a ten-minute talk with Edmonstone on the opposite side of the street from the bank on the forenoon of the day of the murder. He told me that he'd been offered a desk job at Burntisland, but that he preferred to be down below in a boat.'

'Was this on account of Mr Edmonstone suffering from illness in his head, Mr Saunders?'

'I understood that Edmonstone was afraid of seasickness. But on the day of the murder I noticed no change in his appearance or demeanour or mode of talking. When we parted, he said he was catching the tram car, and rushed off.'

Several witnesses, James Goldie, Peter Adamson, Alexander Chalmers, Johnstone Smith, George Clunie and George Black, all testified to having seen Edmonstone and Michael Brown together, around noon, stepping off the tramcar together, then walking along School Wynd. They did not observe anyone else walking close by.

The next witness, Constable Alexander Stewart, described finding Michael Brown's body on the floor of the public lavatory, then visiting Edmonstone's family home that same afternoon, 'We were first told that Edmonstone was suspected between three and four o'clock on the afternoon of the day of the murder. I was informed by his parents that he had gone out in the morning at half past ten and had not yet come back. We then asked his mother for a description of Edmonstone and a photograph of him. His mother went to a box, which was full of photographs, and after a search, she told us that there had been photographs of him in the box and that her son must have removed them all before going out in the morning, as she was unable to find any.'

Constable Stewart then recounted travelling to Manchester, alongside Inspector Peattie, to escort Edmonstone back to Cupar.

'Constable, did the arrested man demonstrate any peculiarity or eccentricity on the journey back to Scotland?'

'No, Sir. He appeared to be depressed, and to feel his position keenly, but it was just the depression of a person against whom such a charge had been made. He answered all my questions sensibly.'

'Thank you, Constable Stewart.'

It was now time for the gruesome medical evidence to be presented.

4 – MANHUNT FOR A MURDERER
(Part Three)

The medical evidence was provided by Dr Alexander Watson:

'From an examination of the scene, it appeared that the struggle had commenced in the urinal outside, and that the boy had been dragged into the closet. I am of the opinion that the cause of death was haemorrhage and shock, probably aggravated by attempts at strangulation. I'm also of the opinion that the wounds described were such as could be caused by blows from a heavy boot or some blunt pointed instrument. The boy had lost a great deal of blood.'

Dr Watson was then shown Edmonstone's boots by Mr Anderson, 'Doctor, could these boots have caused those injuries?'

'The wounds on the deceased correspond very nearly with wounds that would be caused by such boots. I should add that the wounds on the head above the left ear involved considerable violence.'

Mr Anderson, for the Crown then indicated to Lord Guthrie that the prosecution would be calling no further witnesses, satisfied their case had conclusively demonstrated that the accused man, far from being insane at the time of the murder, had carefully, callously, and thoughtfully executed his plan to rob and murder the unfortunate Michael Brown. The onus now lay with Mr Christie, the defence advocate, to prove his client's insanity and save him from the hangman.

The first defence witness, Dr F L Scott, who had been resident physician in Ward 32 at Edinburgh Royal Infirmary in July 1908, recalled a patient from East Wemyss being referred to him: 'Alexander Edmonstone was then twenty-two, and he was complaining of pains in the chest and head. He was also suffering from cerebral spinal irritation. He appeared to be in a state of great pain, and though he was quite conscious, he seemed to be dazed. He had been found on the sands at Buckhaven about ten o'clock at night. When he was admitted to the Infirmary he was in a state of great agitation. He lay in bed on his left side, with his knees drawn up. He kept his head back, and complained about pains in his head and neck. Although there was no swelling or blueness about him at that time, he complained of a great pain when a bright light was thrown upon his eyes. I took his temperature at that time and found it to be 99.6, the normal temperature being 98.4. He was very apathetic, and had a dull heavy appearance. I then placed a hollow needle into his spine and drew off some fluid.'

'Do you think he had full perception of what had happened to him, Doctor?'

'I do not think so.'

'And what conclusions did you draw, Doctor?'

'From a variety of tests on his joints and muscles, I found them to be abnormal, and I located a great tenderness in pressing his spine. There was an eruption at the elbows, wrists, and knees. I made a lumbar puncture which resulted in spinal fluid coming out in greater volume than it ought to have done, which pointed to a distinct abnormality and to some irrational in his cerebral spinal system.'

IN MEMORY OF
MICHAEL SWINTON BROWN
AGED 15 YEARS
DIED 19th FEBRUARY 1909

'What nature of illness was Mr Edmonstone suffering from, Doctor?'

'It was difficult to make an exact diagnosis. I thought he suffered from a nervous disease, although the hospital records described it as "sunstroke", due to his appearance at the time of admission.'

'Tell me, Doctor,' Mr Christie ventured, 'would it affect your opinion if you were informed that since his first episode in July of last year, my client has suffered three more attacks, and was once found lying on the street unconscious?'

'Yes, it would alter it. I should think it would make it more like a case of epilepsy than a case of sunstroke.'

Anderson, the Advocate-Depute, cross-examined Dr Scott at this point: 'Doctor, what consequences do you look for in a patient after sunstroke?'

'Mental disturbances, although these gradually decrease as time passes on.'

Anderson continued the Crown's cross-examination: 'The prisoner is a man of good physique. Was there anything seriously the matter with the man apart from the cerebral spinal abnormality?'

'No.'

'While he was under your charge, did or say anything which would lead you to the conclusion that he was insane?'

'No.'

'Did he say or do anything to make you think he was deficient in mental capacity?'

'I did not look upon him as a patient of high mental capacity, but he was no different from an ordinary individual.'

'Doctor, have you ever diagnosed sunstroke in a patient before?'

'No, I have never seen a case of sunstroke, the disease being very uncommon in this country.'

With the credibility of the doctor virtually destroyed by the prosecution's advocate, Mr Christie quickly dismissed Dr Scott and called his next expert witness, the experienced

Dr Lewis Bruce, from Murthly Lunatic Asylum.

'On 3rd June,' Dr Bruce testified, 'along with Dr Clouston from Edinburgh, I examined the prisoner physically and mentally. I found him to be a well-developed man, with a high, narrow palate, which is normal in a person predisposed to nervous disease. The frontal lobe of the brain rests upon that of the skull above the palate, and if you have a highly arched palate that naturally diminishes the capacity of the skull for containing the brain. I examined Edmonstone's cranium, and found a distinctly painful spot on the left side. The pupils of his eyes were unequal, his hands and facial muscles were tremulous, and his tendon reflexes exaggerated.'

'Doctor, you have heard the evidence as to Edmonstone's previous attacks of illness. On that evidence and on the physical examination which you made in the prison, did you come to any conclusion as to the nature of the illness from which Edmonstone has been suffering during this past year?'

'Yes. I came to the conclusion that on the 21st July 1908, and subsequently, Edmonstone had shown signs of very serious brain disease. From my examination of his mental condition, I concluded that the subject was a degenerate. I thought he was a man of arrested mental development to a mild degree. As to the nature of the illness, I thought he was suffering with epilepsy in July 1908, and since that time.'

'Can you explain, for the court, the effects of epilepsy on a patient's mental condition?'

'The effect of epilepsy on the mental functions is extremely varied. You have cases which go on for years, and the patient is capable of good work and sometimes even a responsible work position. There were other cases of epilepsy where the mental deterioration is pronounced. Where that occurs, they lose self-control, and it impairs their judgment. A degenerate with epilepsy developing in him would mean that such a person would have less self-control. In other words, it might limit his restraint. That would show diminished responsibility. In my opinion, an epileptic patient with a nervous disposition is the most dangerous patient to deal with. They are exceedingly impulsive, and lacking in willpower. They are very easily excited, and show a great deficiency in self-control.'

'Dr Bruce, would you say this was a particularly severe case of epilepsy?'

'Yes, it was a very severe case. Although there were relatively few attacks, the fewness of the attacks has nothing to do with the overall effect it might produce on a man's brain. That depends on the character and nature of the fits, rather than their frequency.'

Once again Mr Anderson, for the Crown, sought to lessen the impact of the defence's expert witness, 'Are the outbursts of epileptics normally suicidal or homicidal, Doctor?'

'No.'

'Did you ever hear of a case where an epileptic owing to his epilepsy carried out a robbery such as you have listened to today, and all apparently premeditated?'

'No, I never had that experience.'

'Tell me Doctor Bruce, does the fact that the accused had not suffered a fit for nineteen days before the boy Brown met his death not alter your opinion?'

'I do not advance the opinion that what took place in the water closet was the result of epilepsy at all.'

'Doctor, have you seen anything in your examination of this man which would induce you to believe that at the time he committed this offence he was completely insane?'

'No, I have no evidence on which I can found an opinion as to his mental state on the 19th February.'

'Would you be prepared to certify him suitable for incarceration in a lunatic asylum?'

'No, I would not certify him for the asylum from what I saw. Epilepsy might also exist in person who is completely sane.'

Now firmly on the back foot, Mr Christie invited his next expert witness, Dr Clouston (an Edinburgh specialist in mental health, and an author of several books on the subject), to explain his findings to the court.

'Dr Clouston, you have also interviewed Alexander Edmonstone. Can you explain your understanding of epileptics to the court?'

'Epileptics, as a class, are the most dangerous of all the inmates at our asylums. If the disease becomes established, you cannot trust such a patient. A considerable number of the murders in Great Britain are committed by epileptics. Mr Edmonstone was especially deficient in self-control, and his reasoning was at fault. I came to the conclusion that Edmonstone's mind had been slightly weakened, and it is my opinion that his responsibility was diminished.

Cunning, in most epileptics and lunatic cases, is the last mental faculty to disappear. Cunning is the primarily protective instinct of all human beings, and is the last to give way. If the patient was epileptic and slightly weakened in the mind, the lowest form of motives would be uppermost in his mind. I am of the opinion that Edmonstone was labouring from a serious disease of the brain.'

Lord Guthrie, attempting to better understand the accused man's condition, asked Dr Clouston some questions of his own: 'Did you see any evidence of a loss of memory in the prisoner?'

'No, your honour. His memory was good; it was very good.'

'Did the prisoner express himself intelligently?'

'Yes, he expressed himself quite clearly. I was able in conversation to form a very fair conclusion as to his mental capacity.'

'Dr Clouston, can you say that Edmonstone, duing the execution of the crime, was moved by the part of his brain which was sane, or the part which was diseased and unsound?'

'I would rather not answer that question.'

So, at 12:30pm on the trial's second day, the defence indicated to Lord Guthrie that they had concluded their case. It was now time for the opposing advocates to deliver their closing addresses to the jury.

Mr Anderson, the Advocate-Depute, spoke first,

'Members of the jury, a peaceful Fifeshire village has been

thrown into a state of horror by the brutal murder of the boy Brown. The victim was a bright young lad of promising career, the pride of his parents.

The prisoner, here, has been proved to be totally sane. One is compelled to liken the case to that of Mr Oscar Slater*. It is not my duty to be vindictive in asking for a verdict on the capital charge, but it is my duty as a public servant to point out that the defence here was a frivolous and unsubstantial case, and I have never heard weaker. I cannot help but contrast this case with that of Oscar Slater, in that both men meant to rob and were met with resistance. One of the worst features of the ruffianly element in this case is that the accused, after taking the money bag, actually stooped down over the breast of the victim and took his watch and chain.

Was that the act of an insane man, I ask you? A so-called insane man who then learnt the difficult task of driving a motor car. I saw nothing in the evidence but sanity, great cunning, and a premediated act, coolly and callously carried out. In this case, I must call for a verdict of guilty of murder!'

For the defence, Mr Christie adopted a more conciliatory tone, while addressing the all-male jury: 'Gentlemen, criminal law is directed against moral guilt, and not against the mere physical act of killing. If, by reason of mental disease and impaired intellect, the crime of which my client is guilty is one of culpable homicide and not of murder. He is little more than a boy, only twenty-three years of age. and yet this is a man, according to the Crown, who is steeped in crime. Mr Edmonstone's motives in hiding the photographs was one of shame and of the affection he felt for his family. Furthermore, his escape was not premediated, but simply a case of the inefficiencies of the local police who allowed him to slip through their fingers. It seems impossible that any jury could send that boy to the gallows,' he paused to point at his client, 'knowing what they now know of his mental condition and circumstances. I submit that you, members of the jury, are bound here to return a verdict of culpable homicide.'

Lord Guthrie, before dismissing the jury, briefly asked them to ignore the reference to the case of Oscar Slater, 'in which between twenty to forty wounds must have been inflicted on the dead Miss Gilchrist. There is no evidence in this case of injuries of a similar nature.'

Alexander Edmonstone did not have long to learn his fate. The jury returned after just ten minutes with a unanimous verdict of 'Guilty of murder as libelled.'

Edmonstone fell back in his chair as Lord Guthrie pronounced his sentence, 'Prisoner at the bar, you have been found guilty of murder. You will be taken from this place to your place of execution, and between the hours of eight o'clock and ten o'clock on the 6th day of July, at the hands of the executioner, you will be hanged by the neck until you are dead. And may God have mercy on your soul. Take him away.'

David Carswell, Edmonstone's solicitor, filed an immediate appeal against the death penalty. However, the Court of Appeal in Edinburgh saw no grounds on which to overturn the conviction, citing that 'the original jury requested no mitigation in their verdict.'

Alexander Edmonstone was executed on the morning of Tuesday, 6 July 1909 at Perth Prison. As the white cap was drawn down over his head by Britain's Chief Executioner, John Ellis, he was heard to utter the words 'May the Lord have mercy on my soul.' It was to be the penultimate execution at Perth Prison before the abolition of capital punishment. The story of the final hanging, almost four decades later, is also featured in this book.

John Ellis – known as 'The Shy Executioner' – would go on to hang over 200 convicted men and women including perhaps the most infamous murderer of the twentieth century, Dr Crippen. After one failed suicide attempt, Ellis eventually took his own life in 1932 by slashing his own neck open with a cut-throat razor.

After an undignified financial disagreement with the Fife Police and the Secretary of State for Scotland, Fife County

Council eventually – and rather begrudgingly – paid the £100 reward to John Atherton, the fellow lodger in Manchester who had first uncovered Edmonstone's whereabouts.

*The case of Oscar Slater, which had concluded just two weeks prior to Alexander Edmonstone's trial, and to which the prosecution referred, had seen the conviction and public vilification of German-Jewish immigrant Oscar Slater for the brutal murder of elderly spinster, Miss Marion Gilchrist. Ironically, thanks to the tireless campaigning of many concerned citizens, including Sir Arthur Conan Doyle, the conviction against Slater would be overturned two decades later, in what was described as 'the greatest miscarriage of justice in Scottish legal history.'

5 - TILL DEATH DO US PART

August 1880 – In Victorian Perth there appears to have been a rash of, what were referred to by the newspapers as *'Wife Murders'*. Whilst the killing of a husband or a child, by a wife or mother, was thought by the public to be truly abhorrent, their attitude towards a husband apparently left with no alternative other than to seek vengeance on a nagging or alcoholic spouse, was somehow treated with a degree of empathy and compassion. In the Victorian and Edwardian eras, a husband's right to expect exemplary behaviour, understanding and devotion from his partner, no matter to what level his own descended, appears to have become an almost inalienable right.

This story of murder from 1880 is one of scores to be referred to the High Court in Perth during the last three decades of Queen Victoria's reign.

On 11 August 1880, Margaret Sturrock was conveyed to Perth Infirmary by her worried neighbours, after she complained of acute pains on the left side of her body. Mrs Sturrock was examined by Dr Howard Bendall, the house surgeon, who diagnosed an inflamed left lung and general poor health. There were no indications of any external injuries or bruising. She explained that a fortnight earlier her husband had 'kicked me on the left side and pushed me, so that I fell onto the corner of a wooden chest.' As the injury had occurred two weeks previously, Dr Bendall assumed that any external bruising from such a collision would have healed naturally. He prescribed a period of rest for Mrs Sturrock and her condition temporarily appeared to rally. Nevertheless, by Monday, 16 August, her condition had worsened again forcing Dr Bendall to dictate a note to the Perthshire Procurator-Fiscal:

'Urgent. Please attend Perth Infirmary to receive and record the deposition of one Mrs Margaret Sturrock. She is the victim of an assault, from the effects of which her life is being despaired of.'

Together with Perthshire Sheriff-Depute Barclay, the Procurator-Fiscal duly took Margret Sturrock's testimony in which she outlined the events leading to her admission, together with providing a list of witnesses. She died from her injuries on Saturday, 21 August and a post-mortem was immediately ordered. In the meantime, a warrant was issued for the arrest of her husband, 48-year-old John Sturrock. He was subsequently indicted as follows:

'On the 31st July last, in your house at Pomarium Street, Perth, you, the accused, did assault and murder Margaret Sturrock, your wife, by striking her several blows on the face and head with his fist. You are further charged with having thrown her upon the floor, and caused her left side to come violently in contact with a chest box, and while she was lying in that position kicked her several times on the left side, whereby she was mortally injured, and died on 28th August last.'

Sturrock pleaded 'Not Guilty' to the charge and a trial date was set for Monday, 13 December at the High Court, leaving the prosecution time to gather witnesses and evidence.

John Sturrock announced that he would be defended by Messrs Rhind and Millie, solicitors of Perth.

The trial of the Crown v John Sturrock opened at the High Court of Justiciary to a packed public gallery.

In the presence of the Lord Justice-Clerk, Lord Moncrieff, Sturrock again entered a plea of 'not guilty' to murder and the evidence for the prosecution began, led by the new Sheriff of Perthshire, John Macdonald and Mr Millie QC.

The first witness, Mrs Hume of Low Street in Perth, testified that:

'On 31st July Mrs Sturrock came to my house between nine and ten with clothes she had been washing. She stayed there for some time. She was quite sober. Mr Sturrock who had been drinking, also called at the house, and when he saw his wife he attempted to strike her.'

'And what happened then, Mrs Hume?'

'Well, sir, my brother, Duncan, was there also and he interfered, saying to Mr Sturrock – "If you are going to strike your wife it will not be here." He then ejected Mr Sturrock from the house. His wife joined him shortly afterwards. They lived in the house opposite mine.'

'And did anything else occur, Mrs Hume?'

'Yes, the next day I heard that Mrs Sturrock was ill, and so I paid her a visit. I found her much swollen about the face.'

At this point Mr Rhind cross-examined on behalf of the defence, 'Mrs Hume, is it true that you gave the deceased a drink when she called at your house that morning?'

'Yes,' stated Mrs Hume in reply, 'she got a mutchkin of drink at my house [a mutchkin was roughly equivalent to three-quarters of a pint]. But she left half of it here when she followed her husband home. The next day I called upon Mrs Sturrock to ask her how her injuries had been inflicted. She replied that her husband had been the cause of them.'

The witness then paused to wave an accusatory finger in the direction of the defendant in the dock. whereupon the accused man cried out 'You're a liar, woman; she fell on the chest.'

After the disruption, Mr Rhind continued his cross-examination of Mrs Hume, 'And did Mrs Sturrock say anything else?'

'No, Sir. But she was coughing a lot.'

The judge interjected at this point to ask a question of his own, 'Had this woman usually a bad cough?'

'No, your honour. She used to smoke, and sometimes she coughed when she was smoking.'

This raised a murmur of laughter in the otherwise tense courtroom before the prosecution summoned their next witness.

'Duncan Campbell, you are the brother of the preceding witness, Mrs Hume. Please describe to the court exactly what took place that morning.'

'Yes, Sir,' Duncan Campbell began, 'I observed that when Mr Sturrock entered my sister's he was wild-like, and he had very fierce-like eyes. He had been at the drink. But his wife was sober when she left.'

The next witness, Annie Munro, a good friend of the victim, asserted that:

'I had known the prisoner's wife for two years previous to her death. On Saturday, 31st July, she was in the grocer's shop about eleven o'clock. She was making purchases there, and appeared to be in perfect health. She asked me to accompany her home, telling me, "My husband is asleep with the drink and, if I awake him, he will kill me." But, when we reached her house, the prisoner was awake and appeared to be very ferocious. After I heard them quarrelling I advised her to turn and leave. She appeared to be in great terror, and attempted to go with me, but her husband followed us. He caught his wife by the throat and gave it a good squeeze. She got away but he continued his pursuit of her.'

John Sturrock, who had been stood passively in the dock until this point in the proceedings laughed out loud and cried out 'Liar!'

After the accused man was admonished by the judge, Annie Moore continued her evidence, 'I saw nothing more of

Mrs Sturrock till next day, when I observed her in bed, with her face much swollen.'

Mrs Easson, the wife of a carpenter, who lived in the flat below the Sturrocks on Pomarium Street, was next in a string of prosecution witnesses to testify, 'On the 31st of July I heard Mr and Mrs Sturrock quarrelling at the foot of the stair leading to their house. I heard him strike his wife twice, and I called out to him "Stop that!" I heard a cry coming from the prisoner's house during that same night, about four o'clock in the morning. It was Mrs Sturrock, she cried out "Murder! Oh, John, John!"'

The evidence from the next witness, Mrs Halley, the wife of a labourer from Carson's Pend, did not seem quite so helpful in establishing the prosecution's case, 'Though I saw Mrs Sturrock frequently after the 31st July, I never heard her blame her husband for knocking her down.'

However, after a great deal of encouragement from the Lord Moncrieff to answer questions more directly, Mrs Halley admitted that 'Mr Sturrock said on Sunday morning that he "had maybe gave my wife a push last night".'

Perhaps the most damaging evidence came from the deceased lady's sister, Mrs Mitchell, who lived in Back Wynd, 'I visited my sister, Margaret, a short time before her death. She complained of a sore side and a bad heart. Afterwards she admitted to me that her husband had given her a push. Then, on 13th August, I visited her at the hospital and found her suffering from a swollen face. When I asked her about it, she stated that the swelling was in consequence of her teeth having been knocked out either by a kick or a blow. She did not blame her husband, then, but remarked that she would never live with him again.'

'Did you take it from this, Mrs Mitchell, that your sister intended to leave her husband?'

'Yes, sir. His feet were as ready as his hands. The last time I visited her at the infirmary she said to me that it was her husband who had assaulted her.'

The final witness, Mr Henderson, a groom who dwelt in the flat above the Sturrocks, testified that:

'Mr Sturrock was drunk on Saturday evening. It was possible he might have struck his wife while she was standing at the foot of the stair. There was a good deal of swearing going on at their home, but I heard no disturbance going on. When I left home at five o'clock on Sunday morning to attend the horses, I called at Sturrock's to see if, as usual, he would accompany me. My wife was worried that he might have murdered her, but I observed Sturrock handing a cup of water to his wife, who was lying ill in bed. They seemed on good terms with each other.'

In cross-examination, Mr Rhind asked Mr Henderson about the deceased lady's general health.

'Scarcely a day went by, sir, when Mrs Sturrock did not take rather more drink than was good for her. She was not a healthy person, and she appeared to be troubled either with asthma or consumption.'

'Thank you, Mr Henderson. No further questions.'

It seemed a lifeline for the defence in a sea of otherwise damaging evidence.

The results of the post-mortem examination made by Dr Bendall and Dr Graham on 28th August found that 'Death was due to inflammation of the left lung and inflammation of the left kidney, both of which might have been caused by external violence on the left side. It is also possible, however, that other unidentified factors might have caused the injury to the kidney. There was nothing in our post-mortem examination to indicate that the deceased was intemperate in her habits. She certainly would not have been unable to work with the inflammation she suffered from.'

The declaration made by Margaret Sturrock on her deathbed was then read to the court:

'I am forty years of age. I have been married for eight years, but have never been very happy, as my husband took drink and abused me when he had. On Saturday, 31st July,

I was engaged running messages to my neighbours, and I locked the house door. This provoked my husband, who was tipsy, and when I returned home he struck me with his fist. He told me he wanted to put me out of the house. I refused to go, whereupon he struck me and caused me to fall on a chest, which caught me on my left side.'

The prisoner's declaration was then read to the jury by the prosecution. In 1880, an accused person was not permitted to testify at their own trial. It was generally felt that this would prejudice their defence, due to the normally low educational standard and unsympathetic nature of most suspects. Although the reading in court of a preprepared statement dictated by the accused person was allowed, it was not compulsory. However, the right to speak in your own defence was introduced in 1883 and extended to cover all offences by 1898.

'I am John Sturrock. I am forty-eight years of age and a carter by profession. On the Saturday night in question I was sober, and had no quarrel with my wife. I did not strike her, knock her down, or kick her. She was not in the house all night, but came in about four o'clock on Sunday morning, having been in Mrs Henderson's house upstairs, all that time. She fell when she came into the house, and I assisted her into bed, and got the doctor next day. I never said to anyone that I had given my wife a push.'

With the evidence for the prosecution concluded, it was time for the defence to present their case.

The first defence witness, John Wilkie, a grocer, deponed that Mrs Sturrock 'visited the shop on that Saturday night about eleven o'clock to buy drink.'

James Halley, whose wife had earlier given evidence on behalf of the prosecution, testified that:

'I have known the prisoner for the last twenty-five years and he has always been of an obliging disposition. For six or seven years after his marriage he appeared to be on good terms with his wife, but in recent years Mrs Sturrock frequently took too much drink. She often complained of her insides, and her chest had been troubled with a cough.'

'And what happened on that Sunday morning, Mr Wilkie?'

'Mr Sturrock came to my house about eleven o'clock and asked me if my wife, Mrs Halley, "could attend Margaret as she has the old sair (sore area) in her side again." He did not say anything else to my wife. Afterwards I saw Mrs Sturrock and she complained that she had hurt herself by falling against the chest. I asked her if her husband had anything to do with it. She told me that he did not.'

John Wilson, a neighbour, confirmed that both 'John Sturrock and his wife were greatly addicted to drink. But he was not violent towards her unless she gave him provocation. The Sturrocks kept a very loose house, but I heard no disturbance on the night in question. In fact, I was at work till four o'clock on Sunday morning, and when I was going home I heard a great disturbance coming from Angus Henderson's house in the garret above the Sturrocks' house.'

'Not *from* the Sturrocks' house?' enquired Mr Rhind.

'No, sir. At that time everything appeared to be quiet in the Sturrocks' house.'

Next the defence called a surprise witness, Dr Nairn, the police surgeon for Perth.

'Can you tell me what happened on the Sunday morning in question, Doctor?'

'Yes. I was called early by the prisoner to attend his wife. When I got to Pomarium Street Mrs Sturrock complained of pain over her left side, which she attributed to having fallen on the corner of a chest. She did not attach any blame to her husband.'

'And did you see the results of the post-mortem examination, Doctor Nairn?'

'Yes. In my opinion, it is difficult to answer definitely whether death was caused by accident, or by the foreign substance which was found in the deceased's kidneys.'

This closed the evidence for the defence and following the

summations by the prosecution and defence advocates, the Lord Justice-Clerk instructed the jury to retire and consider their verdict.

Twenty minutes later the jury returned having reached a decision. By unanimous verdict John Sturrock was found 'not guilty' of murder, but 'guilty' of culpable homicide. As in often the case in Scottish trials, the jury recommended that the court show leniency in their sentencing. The Lord Justice-Clerk intimated that he would pronounce sentence the following morning, after having studied the accused man's previous record – something which, oddly, had not been mentioned during the trial, particularly as one of the defence witnesses has attested to Sturrock's previous good character, a point which would have then allowed the prosecution to challenge that assertion.

Lord Moncrieff before declaring the sentence, informed the court that he would be taking into account the four months Sturrock had already spent on remand in Perth Prison,

'Prisoner at the bar, I have carefully considered the facts of your case, and the verdict of the jury with its recommendation of mercy. The jury have acquitted you of the crime of murder, and reduced their verdict to one of culpable homicide. I think they were right in doing so, because the violence, whatever it was, had an effect beyond anything that you could had expected, seeing that the cause of the woman's death was one of which you were ignorant. I am quite willing to make any allowance for that fact in pronouncing a just sentence upon you. But the jury have found you guilty of culpable homicide, and although they have accompanied their verdict with a recommendation to mercy, I must own that I am not prepossessed in your favour, or in favour of that recommendation, by the facts that came out during this trial. It might be true that the violence you were guilty of towards your wife, whom you had vowed to cherish and protect, was not a violence which, used towards a woman in ordinary health, would have been productive of any serious results; but, on the other hand, I am quite satisfied that the amount of violence used was of a very serious description. The poor woman was in terror of her life during the whole of that night, and it plain from what she said to her friends during her last illness that it was not the first time that she had been in fear of her life. You had lain in wait for her the whole of that night for the purpose of using violence, and at four o'clock in the morning, when she came to her own house, she met her death at your hands. In these circumstances, I am only able to give effect to the recommendation to mercy by abstaining from pronouncing a sentence of penal servitude (hard labour) upon you. The sentence of this Court is that you be imprisoned for eighteen calendar months from the date of your first imprisonment.'

Had the jury known that John Sturrock had at least two previous convictions for robbery with violence, they may not have placed such weight on the evidence of John Wilson, the neighbour who claimed that the disturbance that night had emanated from another house. John Wilson was, in fact, a great deal more than merely a neighbour. He had actually been Sturrock's criminal partner during his two previous criminal escapades, which undoubtedly makes his evidence at this trial prejudiced and unsafe.

To our modern sensibilities, the sympathy attached to the perpetrator of this crime due to the inconvenience of living with his wife's alcoholism, coupled with the fact that he did not appreciate her physical frailties, are difficult to understand. The opinions expressed towards the victim in this trial were all too common in the late nineteenth century. Nevertheless, a woman accused of murdering her alcoholic husband might have expected to be treated in a very different way.

John Sturrock was released ten months later. There is no record of him offending again.

6 – THE MONTROSE MURDER
(Part One)

April 1821 – In the gloomy early hours of Saturday, 28 April 1821, Margaret Shuttleworth, the 36-year-old wife of innkeeper Henry Shuttleworth, disturbed the peace of that early Montrose morning. Cries, followed by the barking of a dog, had already disturbed the neighbours in the narrow close between Bridge Street and Castle Street, where the couple leased the *Hope Inn* from a local brewer, Henry Farquharson, who lived next door.

Around 4am, moments after the unmistakeable sound of another scream, Margaret emerged from the door of the *Hope Inn* and banged loudly on Henry Farquharson's cottage door opposite. Clearly in an agitated state, she blurted out, 'Rise, Farquharson, for Shuttleworth is lying in the entry.'

Margaret informed Farquharson that she had got up in the night to fetch a glass of water from the kitchen downstairs. However, on reaching the bottom of the stairs, she had tripped over something in the dark passageway. After first thinking it was the dog, to her horror, she soon realised it was the body of her husband, Henry. He lay motionless at the foot of the stairwell, his head resting in a large pool of blood. Farquharson quickly dressed and accompanied Margaret next door. The Shuttleworth's maid, Catherine McLeod, was away at the time attending a family wake, meaning Margaret and her husband had been alone in their cottage. Margaret told her neighbour that her husband must have fallen down the stairs in the night, and lamented, 'I wish I heard Henry fall, I might have saved his life.'

Farquharson called Dr Henry Hoile who examined the body. Almost immediately, Dr Hoile realised that Henry Shuttleworth had not died merely from a fall down a flight of stairs and send word to the local town officers, William Bennett and John Shaw, who arrived at daylight to search the Shuttleworths' cramped living quarters. There, in the bedroom on the floor beside the chimney, lay a small poker. Even to the untrained eye, blood and hair were clearly visible on the instrument. Rumours soon spread across the town. Margaret Shuttleworth had already garnered an unsavoury reputation for her violent behaviour – especially when drunk – and only the previous evening her husband had informed Henry Farquharson that he intended to leave his wife and give up the tenancy of the *Hope Inn*, due to his wife's 'drunkenness and cursing.'

Margaret Shuttleworth was arrested and, although she vehemently protested her innocence, she was thrown in the town's jail to await trial. Still a decade before the reign of Queen Victoria, justice in Scotland was harsh and rapid. Without the luxury of forensic evidence, scientific method and modern policing, guilt still depended as much on the accused person's reputation and local gossip, as it did on eyewitnesses and hard evidence. James Patterson, the Burgh Road Surveyor, was employed to prepare a detailed sketch of the premises, as part of the Crown's evidence against Margaret Shuttleworth, and the accused woman was charged by Bailie McGrigor as follows:

'That you, the said Margaret Tindal, or Shuttleworth, are guilty of the said crime, in so far as you did, late on the night of 27th April, or early in the morning of the 28th day of April 1821, did wickedly and feloniously assault Henry Shuttleworth, innkeeper in Montrose and your husband, and did inflict several severe blows upon his head and neck with a poker, or some other instrument to the Prosecutor unknown, whereby his skull was fractured, and he was otherwise mortally wounded; in consequence of which the said Henry Shuttleworth did immediately or soon thereafter die, and was thereby murdered by you.'

The accused woman pled 'not guilty.' On admitting that she could not read or write, her response was noted and a trial date set for 19 September at the Circuit Court of Justiciary in Perth. While Margaret Shuttleworth languished in jail, the authorities now had more than four months to gather evidence against her.

Margaret Tindal had married Henry Shuttleworth in 1804. He was an Englishman and a corporal in the Royal Marines at the time. The couple had met while Henry was 'pressganging' for the Army in Montrose. Margaret was, by all accounts, beautiful and had been born in Gothenburg, Sweden, in 1785, before moving to Scotland. The couple relocated wherever Henry was billeted, until finally moving to Montrose after he was released on a half-pay pension at the conclusion of the Napoleonic Wars.

After a failed attempt to run a small grocery shop on North Road, and the occasional foray into the smuggling business, Henry took on the lease of the *Hope Inn* from Henry Farquharson. However, it seems the couple drank heavily and argued often. Margaret was frequently abusive and aggressive towards her husband, and the couple no longer shared a bedroom. Mr Shuttleworth slept in the bedroom above the inn and his wife in the room downstairs. In a recent argument, a furious Margaret had smashed the kitchen window, for which Henry Shuttleworth was charged the sum of seven pence to repair. This had created yet more friction between the bickering couple.

If the nineteenth-century's legal system already appeared skewed against the accused person, its attitude towards a drunken woman, especially one charged with killing her own husband, was harsh in the extreme.

By today's more liberal standards, justice in the late nineteenth century seems cruel. However, it appears positively progressive compared to that meted out in the 1820s. If Margaret Shuttleworth had needed any reminder of that fact, as she sat in her lockup on the morning of her trial, she merely needed to glance through the bars of her cell at the defendant in the other case due to appear in Perth Court that day. A middle-aged man by the name of William McDonald had already been 'paraded and whipped' through the streets of Perth, before pleading 'guilty' to the 'theft of a pocket handkerchief and of being by habit and repute a thief.' He was sentenced to 'transportation to the colonies for a period of fourteen years.' The Right Honourable David Boyle, the Lord Justice Clerk, and Lord Pitmilly, were clearly in no mood for leniency. Margaret Shuttleworth could only hope they would be softened by the appearance of a woman at the bar.

Mr Maconochie, His Majesty's Depute Advocate, prosecuted on behalf of the Crown, and Margaret Shuttleworth was defended by Robert Thomson from Edinburgh.

As was always the case during the nineteenth century, the appearance of a woman in court, notably when facing a charge of murder, created huge public interest. Several newspapers, including the *Caledonian Mercury*, tapped into this fascination by commenting at length on Margaret's appearance and demeanour:

'About twelve o'clock the prisoner was brought to the bar, dressed in a fashionable black bonnet and net plain muslin cap, her hair tastefully dressed in small ringlets on each side of her forehead, a black gown and scarlet shawl, with a gold broach on her breast, on her fingers were several rings, she looked remarkably well. By the excessive heat in the court she seemed to be much incommoded, and at their Lordships' suggestion took off her bonnet, and several times during the trial she was offered some soup. Upon being requested to stand up for the purposes of being identified, she did so promptly and did not seem at all embarrassed.'

James Patterson, the Burgh Road Surveyor, provided the court with a detailed plan of the Hope Inn. Constructed over two floors, the building had a 'shop' (public bar), room, and kitchen on the ground floor, and adjacent living accommodation in an upper flat. In answer to the prosecution's request for a description of the building's aspect and security, Mr Patterson referred to the careful diagrams he had created: 'The shop fronts onto Castle Street, the house enters from a passage leading from Castle Street to Bridge Street. A window from the kitchen on the ground floor looks into that passage. A window from Mrs Shuttleworth's bedroom looks into Collector Parson's property on the north. On the right hand of the stair to the upper flat is a door into the shop, on the left, a door to Mrs Shuttleworth's bedroom. All the doors had locks and bolts except the one onto Castle Street, which had a sneck or lifter opening from the inside. From a hole under the sneck, it might possibly be opened from the outside. I also understand that the passage is kept open for the brewery all day, then shut at night.'

While this evidence might have given the defence some hope, by suggesting an unknown person may have been able to gain entry through the door leading to Castle Street, the testimony of Mr Farquharson the landlord painted a much blacker picture of the scene that night:

'I know the deceased and his wife were on very bad terms. Henry Shuttleworth gave me notice that he was going to give up his premises on account of his wife's behaviour, he told me this the night before he was found dead. It was half-past ten when I left their home to return to mine and I saw no other person in the Shuttleworth's house. I also heard no person enter the house after I left him, and no noise or disturbance whatever. About four o'clock in the morning, Mrs Shuttleworth came across to my house, and said, "Rise, Farquharson, for Shuttleworth is lying in the entry." I got up, and found him lying in the passage, by the back door; he was dead and cold. I said I would go for a doctor, to which she made no objections.

I brought Dr Hoile; who observed blood marks on the stair; there were also finger marks of blood on the kitchen door, about 3 feet from the ground. Dr Hoile examined the pockets of the deceased, and found seven shillings and some copper. We also found the key of the shop-door and opened it, nothing appeared to have been taken out; a quantity of money was still in the desk.'

'And what about the position of the deceased man's body, Mr Farquharson?' enquired Maconochie, His Majesty's Depute Advocate.

'I do not think that by Shuttleworth falling downstairs he could have been in the position I saw him.'

At this point, Maconochie reminded the jury that Margaret Shuttleworth had previously been interrogated regarding the blood marks on the stairway, to which she had claimed, 'I had been up there looking for the servant girl.'

The medical testimony of Dr Hoile and Dr Cramb (who had assisted with the post-mortem) seemed to further the Crown's cause:

'I was called to examine the body of Shuttleworth, at four o'clock in the morning. I found it lying as previously described. There was a wound on the back part of the head; the skull was fractured. The wounds appeared to have been occasioned by some ponderous body having struck the head, which appeared to be some blunt weapon. The fracture at the back of the head could not have been from a fall. It must have been occasioned by several blows; three blows I could distinctly count, from the extravasation of blood from the wounds. Whilst examining the body, I saw the prisoner, who came from the bedroom. I then went upstairs to examine the room, and it appeared some person had lain there.'

'And was the prisoner there at this time, Dr Hoile?'

'Yes, she was. I asked Mrs Shuttleworth if she had been upstairs after she found her husband's body. She said she had not, but immediately corrected herself, saying. "I had been up looking for the servant girl." Her hands had the mark of blood, particularly the forefingers.'

'And did you enquire as to the reason for this, doctor?'

'No. I did not ask her to account for these appearances as she seemed to be confused and ashamed of being intoxicated. However, I noticed one spot of blood on her blue check apron, which was lying on a chair. I also observed several marks of blood on the wall to the right of the house door, opposite the staircase. I saw blood on the bolt of the outer door also.'

'And was blood present on the victim, doctor?'

'I did observe some marks of blood on the legs of the deceased man. As I previously stated, the fractures could not possibly have arisen from a fall downstairs. I think that a poker used broadwise might have occasioned the wound on the victim's head. In addition, where the wounds were, the hair seemed to be off.'

The medical evidence regarding the poker appeared conclusive too. Dr Hoile and William Bennett (who had arrived at the *Hope Inn* on the morning after the discovery of the body) both identified the poker shown to them in court, as the one found on the floor close to the body of Henry Shuttleworth. William Bennett described the exhibit:

'The poker was slightly bent at one end. There was hair on it. Short, thin, and light-coloured. Shuttleworth's hair was light. I thought the hair on the poker looked like the hair on the lower part of Shuttleworth's head, near his neck.'

Interestingly, however, although Dr Cramb corroborated much of Dr Hoile and William Bennett's testimony, he declared that 'I examined the poker, but did not see anything upon it.'

The case against Margaret Shuttleworth, although circumstantial by modern standards, already seemed sufficient to guarantee a conviction. Nevertheless, the final three witnesses for the Crown all but made certain.

Elizabeth Craw had visited the Shuttleworth's neighbour, Mr Farquharson, on the evening before the murder:

'Between seven and eight I heard a pane of glass break. I went down and Henry Shuttleworth was walking on the pavement, his wife was still within the house. Mr Shuttleworth shouted to his wife, "Come down, woman, and see what you have done!" She came out and looked at the window; then went in and shut the door. She shouted, "If I had the big poker I would lay your brains on the floor and let you look at them!" I thought she was the worse for liquor. Later, I heard a dog barking, but I cannot say whether it was Mr Shuttleworth's dog. I think it was after eleven o'clock that I heard it.'

Jane McDonald testified to visiting the *Hope Inn* on the same evening in the hope of finding some lodgings for her brother, 'Mr Shuttleworth,' she attested, 'said, 'sorry, I cannot take in a stranger. On account of my wife being worse for liquor. I am in danger of my own life from her," he told me.'

Conceivably the most damaging evidence of all came from Catherine McLeod, the Shuttleworths' maid, whose testimony demonstrated a clear bias against the accused woman, for whom she clearly had little affection. Indeed, it has been commented that she 'carried a torch' for the murdered man – perhaps even enough to possess a motive of her own. Nevertheless, it is doubtful that any of the fifteen male jurors (who all undoubtedly employed servant girls of their own) questioned the witness's objectivity.

'I came into Mr Shuttleworth's service at Martinmas,' Catherine McLeod testified. [Martinmas, celebrated on 11th November, was one of the traditional Scottish 'Quarter Days' on which new contracts of employment, or rent, were entered into or terminated. The traditions of the 'Feast of St Martin' often included the killing of a goose or fowl, followed by the drawing of the animal's blood, into which a piece of flax would be dipped.]

Catherine McLeod continued:

'I remained in his service from Martinmas until his death. There was no other person living in the house, except Mr Shuttleworth, his wife, and me. Mr Shuttleworth and his wife, my mistress, were very happy when she was sober; but she was often drunk, and then she was very outrageous with her tongue, cursing and swearing.'

'Do you recognise this poker?' asked Mr Maconochie, brandishing the exhibit for dramatic effect.

'Yes, sir. I know the poker, which belonged in the kitchen. I have seen her...' Catherine McLeod stopped in mid-sentence to point accusingly at the defendant, 'I have seen her throw the poker after her husband in the passage. When he died on the night between Friday and Saturday, I did not see the poker at that time. On the Friday afternoon Mrs Shuttleworth was intoxicated, and desired me to buy some tobacco for her; but I refused, as my master did not want me too. It was the market day, and several people were in the house. I was sent on an errand, and, on coming back, I found my master sitting at the kitchen fireside. My mistress was also in the kitchen. Some words passed between them, after which he went out. My mistress then drove her hand through the kitchen window and was outrageous. Their quarrel became greater after this. When I went out with the empty bottles, as usual, she was lying on the floor. I put her to bed, as she was completely intoxicated. I then asked permission from the master to go to a late wake, for Mr Farquharson's niece, who had just passed away. He consented; but bade me first undress my mistress. My mistress and her husband had slept in separate beds for a long time previous.'

There would be more to come from the clearly disgruntled maid.

7 - THE MONTROSE MURDER
(Part Two)

Catherine McLeod continued her testimony, clearly relishing her moment in the limelight:

'I shut the shop between nine and ten that night and went to the wake, and I did not return till half-past three the next morning, when Mrs Farquharson came for me, and told me that my master had fallen downstairs. When I came home, the inside door was open, and there were people at it. My master's head was lying near the foot of the stair. Dr Hoile, Mr. Farquharson, and my mistress were there.'

'And how did your mistress appear?'

'The drink appeared to be somewhat off her, by then, Sir. My mistress was dressed then too, although she had no apron on when I saw her, but had one on the night before. She told me that she was going into the kitchen for a drink, and she fell over something, which she thought was the dog; she bowed down and felt the face of her husband. Then she said that she went upstairs first to look for me, not knowing that I had gone to the late wake, then she told me that she went to fetch Mr Farquharson.'

'Thank you, Miss McLeod. And returning to the matter of your deceased master, what did you observe in the dwelling?'

'When I saw my master lying there, he had on his waistcoat, breeches, and stockings. There were footmarks on the stair leading to the bedroom. I saw also some marks on the door, but noticed no blood on the passage from the kitchen to the room. There was only a poker and fender in that room. The poker you have shown me is the same one, it was found under a desk in the shop. It was cracked, it had been so for some time. I saw no marks of violence on the doors or windows of the house, but the shutter of the kitchen window was open when I got there, although someone must have shut it by the time I went away. I did not notice anything amissing out of the house.'

'And did your master ever talk to you of his troubles?'

'Yes, sir. Several times. He talked often of leaving Montrose; but this talk made his wife angry.'

'And did your mistress say anything else to you when you first returned from the wake?'

'Yes. When I went to first open the door, my mistress was behind it. She appeared troubled. She said, "I wished I had heard him fall, as I might have saved his life." She also said to me that she was "past crying" and that she had "no wish to have the body removed or a doctor sent for." I also saw a candlestick in my master's bedroom and some marks on the stair that appeared to be made by a small bare foot, but I'm not certain whether my mistress had shoes on or not.'

With the prosecution now finished, the advocate for the defence, Mr Thomson, now began his attempt to save Margaret Shuttleworth, who was not permitted to speak in court (although the reading of a pre-agreed declaration on her behalf was permitted). To make matters worse, the already hamstrung defence had already been severely handicapped after a number of highly damaging editorials were published in several newspapers, long before the trial had even begun. Headlines such as this no doubt influenced even the most neutral of jurors:

'When taken to prison, on the Sunday morning at nine o'clock, she was undismayed, asserted her innocence, and perhaps the most striking feature in her behaviour then was not her declaration of conscious innocence, nor her drunkenness, but no lamentation over, or apparent sorrow for, the untimely death of her husband.'

Returning to the trial, Mr Thomson first assured the court that Mrs Shuttleworth was of sound mind and not under the influence of drink when making her original statement. He then proceeded to address the jury:

'The following declaration was made at Montrose, the thirtieth day of April, one thousand eight hundred and twenty-one years, in the presence of Mr John McGrigor, one of the present Bailies of the Burgh of Montrose, "That, I, Margaret Tindal, widow of Henry Shuttleworth, vintner in Montrose, who being examined, declare that, I was married upwards of fifteen years ago; and that we have lived for the last five years in Montrose, four years whereof my husband has kept an inn, in the house formerly occupied by Henry Farquharson; that we lived pretty comfortably together as man and wife; that we sometimes had words, but never came to blows; that on the evening of Friday last, the twenty-seventh current, I went to bed betwixt nine and ten o'clock; that I and my husband have not slept together for about two months past, my husband having a small bedroom upstairs, and that I slept in the ground flat; that there was a maid servant in the house of the name of Catherine McLeod, who, on the evening of Friday last, asked liberty from my husband, to attend the late wake of a niece of Henry Farquharson, our landlord, on the Bridge Road.

I left my husband and the maidservant in the house when I went to bed. When I awoke between three and four o'clock of the Saturday morning, and came out of my own room to go to the kitchen for a drink of water or small beer; that when I came out of my room I trod upon something, which I thought was the dog, in the passage, but upon feeling with my hand, I found my husband lying on the floor with his feet towards her room door, and his head towards the door which is the access to the front shop from the passage; that I went to the kitchen to call the servant girl, but finding she was not in the house, I went upstairs in search of her. I did not find the servant girl upstairs, and afterwards I came down. I attempted to raise my husband; but finding that he was dead, I opened the door, which was barred, and went to awaken Mr Farquharson, who lives in the opposite side of the close, and James Craw, who lives next to Mr Farquharson; that they came along and they carried the body into the low room; that he was lying on his back when I found him in the passage, and there was a good deal of blood on the floor; that the shop door where his head was lying, was locked; that Dr Hoile was sent for to examine the body, and see whether anything could be done for my husband. The servant girl was also sent for. I had no words of anger with my husband during Friday or the evening of that day".'

Mr Thomson reminded that court that Margaret Shuttleworth was unable to read or write, but had 'made her mark upon the bottom of the document' and 'declared it to be the truth.'

On the day following her initial declaration, Margaret Shuttleworth had amended her statement, adding:

'I declare that although there were some high words between my husband and me on Friday afternoon last, there was no particular quarrel between us; that I went to bed that night at half-past nine o'clock, and never again saw my husband until I found him lying dead at the stair foot in the morning; that no pane of glass was broke in the house on that Friday afternoon or evening, but as farmers and country people are constantly going out and in on that day, which is the market day at Montrose, I cannot recollect all that happens. When I discovered my husband on Saturday morning, at the foot of the stairs, I thought he was asleep, and put down my hands to raise up his head; by that means they were stained with the blood which had flowed from his head, and I was so much stupefied and engaged that I had no time to wash the blood off before Dr Hoile came in, all of which I declare to be the truth.'

With the formality of the defence's testimony completed, the evidence was summed up for the jury by the Lord Justice Clerk:

'I consider this case as one of a very important nature,' he began, 'which depends on evidence of an entirely circum-stantial nature, a case in which you, the jury, will have to weigh all the evidence brought before you. I consider the case in two points. First, whether the deceased lost his life by violence, or by accident, and second, if his death was by violence, whether the accused at the bar is guilty of that crime. If it should be thought by you that the death arose solely from an accident, it will be unnecessary to waste the time of this court any further; but if, on the contrary, it should appear that he met his death by violence, it is for you to consider how far the accused is implicated in that violence.'

It was now ten o'clock at night, and the Lord Justice Clerk took the unusual step of allowing the jury to retire overnight to consider their verdict, with an instruction to return at ten o'clock the following morning with their verdict. Meanwhile. Margaret Shuttleworth was returned to her cell to await their decision.

The fifteen jurors duly returned at ten o'clock sharp with a unanimous verdict of 'guilty.' The Lord Justice Clerk thanked the jury for the close attention they had paid to the evidence given during the trial, and was 'happy that you have agreed entirely with the opinion expressed by myself and Lord Pitmilly.' He then addressed Margaret Shuttleworth:

'Prisoner at the bar, an intelligent jury have, in one voice, found you guilty of the murder of your husband. It now only remains for me to award that punishment which the law lays down for your crime. Murder, more especially by the wife of her husband is alike forbidden by both the laws of man and God. You will be taken back to the Tolbooth of Perth, to be therein detained and fed on bread and water, until the 1st day of November next, and then to be carried to the Tolbooth of Montrose, and then to be hanged on the 2nd day of said month, between two and four o'clock, at any place the Magistrates of the Burgh should choose, and your body given to Dr Alexander Munro of Edinburgh, to be publicly dissected and anatomized. Take the prisoner away.'

Hanging was not seen as a sufficient enough punishment for this most heinous of crimes, under the terms of the Murder Act 1752. In order to heap further humiliation on the families of the guilty party, and to dissuade others from committing a similar offence, bodies were often publicly gibbeted or dissected (also robbing the relatives of a chance to bury their loved ones). Dissection also offered nineteenth-century scientists the opportunity to study the 'criminal brain', which was thought to differ in some way from the mind of a 'normal citizen'.

However, before Margaret Shuttleworth could be hanged and dissected, there was still time to lodge an appeal against her conviction. The term 'appeal' in the modern legal sense did not apply in 1821. No Court of Appeal existed. An appeal simply meant a plea to the authorities for mercy.

After her sentencing, Margaret Shuttleworth's behaviour changed noticeably. Without access to liquor she mellowed and whiled away the long hours in deep conversation with the warder's wife and with the prison chaplain, who both read to her at length. She declared, 'I am perfectly ignorant of how my husband met his fate; I know nothing of it. I have no doubt I will suffer now, but I will die innocent of the crime.'

Despite her fortitude and acceptance of the verdict, there were enough concerned citizens in the Burgh of Montrose to compile a petition of 200 signatures against her forthcoming execution:

'Unto his most excellent Majesty George the Fourth, by the grace of God, the petition of the undersigned inhabitants of the Royal Burgh of Montrose:

Far be it for your humble petitioners to impugn the sentence of this High Court, but we humbly beg leave to represent to your Majesty that the verdict proceeded entirely upon circumstantial evidence, and there is a strong possibility that the deed may not have been committed by this unhappy convict, who continues to declare herself innocent of the crime of which she had been found guilty. She was the first to give the alarm, and behaved in every respect in the way that a person in her situation, unconscious of guilt, would have done. Although a day elapsed before she was apprehended, she made no attempt to conceal herself, or to escape from justice, and she wished the funeral of her husband delayed, so as every inquiry might be made as to the cause of his death.

The petitioners think, under these circumstances, that the ends of justice might be satisfied by the substitution of any punishment short of death.'

Margaret Shuttleworth dictated a plea of her own, in which she claimed that 'A person of the name of ---------- had stated that he had been in the neighbourhood of the *Hope Inn* on the night the murder was committed, and that he heard noise from within the house, and that he went to the door – which was mentioned by other witnesses as having been shut. This person pledged himself to come forward in my defence at my trial, but he disappeared in a mysterious manner. I was therefore deprived of the benefit of his evidence, which would, no doubt, have operated to my advantage.'

The man's name was redacted from her plea for clemency after the person in question was located and questioned but denied any knowledge of this incident, despite the following claim, made by the unknown man's wife, which seems to implicate him, and which was subsequently reported in the *Montrose Chronicle*:

'The wife is said to have declared that her husband was absent on the night the murder was committed, and that he came in with bloody hands at five o'clock on the following morning. When interrogated he confessed to being in Shuttleworth's house along with his half-brother, who is a smuggler of whisky; that he spoke about it through his sleep, and afterwards left the town. This individual has since returned. He utterly denies the charge brought against him.'

The mysterious man was never publicly named.

Nevertheless, despite this astonishing revelation and the

petition, the sentence of execution was not commuted. A respite of one month was granted by William Hamilton, the Sheriff Depute of Forfar, 'granted only for the purposes of making further enquiries into the circumstances of the case.'

This re-examination of the witnesses and evidence took place in secret, and its results were never published. Whether a detailed scrutiny of the evidence ever really took place, we will never know. No reprieve arrived for Margaret Shuttleworth, despite a further petition for leniency being signed by 'thirty persons of the greatest respectability, clergymen, gentlemen, and opulent householders', and sent to Lord Sidmouth (the Home Secretary and former Prime Minister). The date for Margaret Shuttleworth's execution was fixed for 7 December 1821.

A crowd of 4,000 gathered in Montrose on the appointed day, despite the stormy conditions, to witness Margaret Shuttleworth pinioned on the gallows. Once in position, the condemned woman was given a last chance to confess her guilt.

'Are you guilty of the murder of your late husband?'

'I am not.'

'Then, as a dying woman, do you declare yourself innocent of the crime charged against you?'

'I am innocent, so help me God, I loved my husband as I loved my life.'

The noose was placed forcefully around her neck by Mr Mill, the hangman, so tightly that she gasped out, 'Ye're choakin' me already, and I have something more to say.'

The pressure of the rope was relaxed enough to allow her to exclaim, 'Lord have mercy on me. I die an innocent woman. I am ignorant of, and innocent of the death of Henry Shuttleworth. Drinking has brought me to my ruin.'

A handkerchief was placed in Margaret's right hand, and she was instructed to drop it at the moment she felt ready to 'drop into eternity.' This she did, shortly after her final words, and the executioner crashed his axe down on the cord supporting the beam which bore her weight. An official record of the execution, *The Trial of Margaret Tindal, alias Shuttleworth,* published shortly after, recorded the event in gruesome detail:

'Two feet ten inches of rope had been allowed for her to drop, and it is probable that the victim of the law never felt a pang. The hand that dropt the napkin was never closed, nor did she appear to suffer. Two  minutes after the drop fell, she was hoisted up by the rope and pulleys to be in full view. Though not suffering, Mrs Shuttleworth was not dead for six minutes – the soul unwilling to leave its earthly tabernacle, still lingered, unwilling to quit the situation which that merciful God, who gave it had assigned; but at four minutes past three a last convulsive quiver was noticed.

Seeing Mrs Shuttleworth now suspended, a lifeless corpse, it may be noticed that she was about 36 years of age, small, neat, and good looking, a face inclined to but not absolutely pale, with a slight obliquity of vision. To those who did not see her, the best idea of her appearance on the scaffold may be conceived by imagining a woman in the middle rank of life, expecting a visitor to breakfast, her cap was a morning one, with a handkerchief tied round her head, cleanly dressed in black clothes, a frill round her neck, black stockings, new boots and black gloves.'

Margaret Shuttleworth's body was taken down at 6pm and transported to Dr Munro's Anatomical School in Edinburgh. Following the dissection, Dr Munro noted, 'that the only peculiarity worth noticing was the extremely soft composition of the brain.'

She was the last woman to be publicly executed in Montrose.

And there the story should end, were it not for an astonishing revelation printed in several newspapers almost a decade later. A private letter, written by a man on the eve of his own execution in London during the summer of 1830, confessed to being 'the sole murderer of Margaret Shuttleworth's husband.' The account, published in June 1830, is scant in detail and reports only that the man has 'just now been executed.' After some research, it seems the only recorded hanging of a man in London during the weeks preceding this newspaper report, occurred on 14 April 1830, when Thomas Sales was executed at Newgate Prison for burglary, It was known that Sales had operated with a gang of burglars for many years. Had he really been in Montrose nine years earlier, perhaps taking advantage of a busy market day, to steal from the *Hope Inn*, only to be disturbed by Henry Shuttleworth?

To suddenly confess to a seemingly unconnected nine-year old murder certainly seems a peculiar thing to do, unless of course, he wished to unburden himself before facing the hangman's noose. It is a sobering thought.

8 – THE DOUBLE CHLOROFORM MURDER
(Part One)

Saturday, 4 July 1959 – marked the beginning of a prolonged spell of warm weather in Scotland. Schoolchildren made the most of their summer holidays and played outside with their friends in the fields and streets, often spending the whole day outside, finally returning home as dusk fell, exhausted.

Sixteen-year-old William Kidd, and his two younger siblings (Patricia aged twelve and Graham, aged ten), were much the same. They had spent the weekend away at friends in Dunblane and were dropped off at the end of the lane close to their home, around 8pm on the Sunday evening. A small group of the children's friends accompanied them. It was still light as they crossed the tracks and flat fields leading to their parents' home on the Balcomie Castle Farm Estate, a mile or so from the village of Crail in Fife. The isolated cottage lay on Scotland's east coast, close to the peninsula at Craighead, where the cooling breezes of the North Sea meet the mainland. The children lived in one of the four semi-detached farm cottages at the end of the secluded road, just past the impressive Balcomie Castle Farmhouse. Beyond the cottages, the track petered out into the fields and to the sea beyond. Visitors seldom travelled so far from the beaten track. It was idyllic, remote and peaceful. A peace about to shattered by a horrific discovery.

William Kidd, the oldest of the group of children, knocked on the door of the family's cottage several times but received no answer. He thought it unusual that neither of his parents, nor his fourteen-year-old sister (who had decided to remain at home that weekend) seemed to be at home. Their father's distinctive 1935 Hillman Minx was not outside the house. The car's rear windows were covered in colourful pennants collected from the family's many trips around the country, making it easily noticeable.

The door to the house was locked and William had not taken a key with him, as his parents had assured him that they would be at home when the children returned on Sunday evening. Eventually, he decided to climb in through in a narrow window and unlock the door from the inside, to let the others in. Once inside, he looked for the spare front door key, but it did not seem to be in its usual place. Luckily, William was able to open the door from the inside, using a screwdriver from the kitchen drawer, and let the other children inside. William was a sensible and mature lad, who was just about to begin an electrician's apprenticeship. He made a cup of tea for the group and began to chop some wood for the fire. Eventually, as the shadows lengthened, the other children left for their own homes leaving the siblings alone. Unusually, their beds had not been made – a task their mother had always attended to religiously. The messiest bed of all seemed to be their parents' double bed. The blankets and pillows seemed unnaturally dishevelled and lumpy. William nervously and slowly lifted one of the pillows. To his horror, underneath the pillow was the pallid, unmoving face of his mother. One half of her face had been covered in a cloth; the other was heavily bruised. William shouted out 'Mum, mum!', but she did not answer. He touched her arm, which was now rigid and cold. Then he turned and ran to the neighbour's cottage for help.

His mother's body was alone in the house, his father and sister were nowhere to be seen.

The police were soon called and arrived around 9.20pm on that Sunday evening, together with a surgeon who confirmed that Mrs Kidd appeared to have died from asphyxiation. Detective Superintendent David Brice from Kirkcaldy took charge of the investigation and immediately questioned the Kidd's next-door neighbour. He was able to inform the detective that he had heard the unmistakable sound of Kidd's pre-war Hillman Minx driving off at 4.30am that morning.

Meanwhile, earlier that same Sunday afternoon, and 42 miles away, on Lord Bruce's Broomhall Estate near Dunfermline, gamekeeper Alexander Forrester had been patrolling the grounds in a copse close to the Kincardine-Rosyth Road. when he noticed a large pile of leaves. Mr Forrester had walked past that same spot the previous day and the leaves had not been there. He decided to investigate. The area was often used by picnickers and courting couples, so he was accustomed to finding the ground in that particular spot disturbed. However, nothing could have prepared him for the shock he received as he parted the leaves to reveal the motionless body of a young girl. By the scratches on the girl's face, it was clear that she had fought her attacker and struggled violently before being killed.

Dr Angus Morris, the Dunfermline Police Surgeon, was quickly able to confirm that the girl's death had been 'caused by smothering, probably on the previous day', and that she 'had been involved in a struggle before death.' The identity of the girl was unknown at that stage and Fife's second murder investigation in as many days was launched when Dunfermline Police released a plea for public assistance:

'The body of a girl has been found hidden under a pile of leaves in a copse at the Broomhall estate of the Earl of Elgin, approximately three miles from Dunfermline. The girl was wearing a homemade cardigan and a blouse imprinted with the names of rock 'n' roll stars like Elvis Presley and Tommy

Steele. The body was found by a gamekeeper at a spot just off the main coast road from Fife to Glasgow. The gamekeeper, Mr Alexander Forrester, believes that the body had been placed there during Saturday night or early on Sunday. This area is used by courting couples at all times of the day and we urge anyone who may have seen something to come forward and contact the police.'

Returning to the scene of Christina Kidd's murder at Balcomie Farm Cottages, Detective Superintendent Brice issued a statement of his own to the press:

'The police wish to trace William Dowie Dalgety Kidd, aged thirty-five, tractor foreman, husband of Mrs Kidd, and father of their missing daughter. He is five feet six inches tall and has blue eyes, light brown hair brushed straight back, a tanned complexion, possibly dressed in a dark blue suit, with blue shirt and collar attached. He is thought to be in driving a 1935 model black Hillman Minx saloon car, registration CMH 5I7. This car has pennants and flags completely covering the rear window and rear offside and nearside windows.'

The distinctive description of the young girl's blouse quickly established that the young girl's body discovered on the Broomhall Estate was that of Christina Kidd (junior), the fourteen-year-old daughter of William Kidd and Christina Kidd. The police were now seeking a double murderer. DS Brice responded accordingly:

'It has been established that the body of the young woman found near Dunfermline is that of Christina Kidd, aged fourteen, of Balcomie Farm Cottages, Crail, Fife. At about 9.20pm yesterday, the body of Christina Kidd Senior, the girl's mother, was found in a bedroom at the cottage. Death in each case is thought to be due to asphyxia. A post-mortem examination is being carried out.'

The description of William Kidd (senior) and his distinctive car was repeated, and the public warned:

'This man may be dangerous. In the meantime, the police are treating this as a double murder.'

It would not be long before a number of witnesses came forward. Around 5.30am on the Sunday morning (approximately an hour after William Kidd's neighbour had heard him drive away from Balcomie Farm Cottages), John Flockhart noticed the Hillman Minx parked on the side of the road in Kirkcaldy. As he walked past the car the driver spoke to him:

'I've run out of petrol. Do you know where there's a garage?'

Flockhart replied 'Yes.' As he bent down to give the man directions, he noticed a young girl sitting on the front passenger seat, her head slumped back, apparently asleep. The driver noticed and explained that his young companion was 'dead beat.'

Two hours later, around 7.30am, James Ellis was passing the copse where young Christina Kidd's body would be discovered later that day, when he noticed an old Hillman Minx car being reversed out onto the road, from a clearing in the trees. He could see inside the vehicle clearly and noticed only a man driving. There did not appear to be anyone else in the car.

A few minutes later, and five miles further west on the same road, David Inglis was walking to work when the driver of an old Hillman Minx pulled up alongside him and offered him a lift to Kincardine. According to Inglis, 'the driver said he was going on a camping holiday and appeared quite normal. There was no one else in the car.'

From the general direction in which Kidd appeared to be travelling, it was assumed he was either heading for Glasgow or perhaps for England. A nationwide description of both the car and its driver was circulated to police stations, and transport cafes across the country. With Britain's first section of motorway recently opened, and the new M1 due to be completed shortly, faster car journey times to England now meant that Kidd might already be many miles away.

Another 48 hours would pass until William Kidd's car was finally spotted by a lorry driver in Worcestershire, almost 400 miles from Fife. Malvern Police were informed, who then managed to trace the suspect to a fruit-picking farm nearby. He was arrested by Constable Frederick Hill, and returned to Fife to be questioned. Kidd was then arraigned before Sheriff Prain at a special hearing in Perth and charged:

'On Saturday 4th, or Sunday 5th July, in your house at Balcomie Farm, you did assault your wife, Christina Duff Graham Harvey or Kidd by administering chloroform to her, holding an unknown object over her face, asphyxiating her and did murder her. And that in that same house or elsewhere in Fife you did assault your daughter, Christina Kidd, by administering chloroform to her, holding an object over her face, asphyxiating her and did also murder her.'

An advocate, Mr Douglas Reith QC, was appointed to represent William Kidd and a trial date set for 20 October 1959 at the High Court in Perth. Reith indicted that the defence would be entering a special plea of 'not guilty on the grounds that the defendant was insane at the time he was alleged to have committed the crimes.'

The *St Andrews Citizen* newspaper also reported that 'The police have collected a total of eighty-three prosecution witnesses for the trial. Mrs Christina Kidd, was a mother of four, originally from Perth. The Kidd family moved from Strathmiglo just three months prior to the tragedy. Young Christina Kidd, it has been disclosed, celebrated her fourteenth birthday just a few days earlier, and was a popular pupil of Waid Academy in Anstruther.'

A recent change to the law in the Scotland, coupled with the unusual method of murder employed in this case, and the technicalities surrounding Kidd's 'not guilty' plea, would make this one of the most anticipated trials ever to take place at the High Court in Perth.

Growing public distaste with capital punishment had led to a recent royal commission recommending changes to the criminal law which governed the death penalty. In the years prior to the case of The Crown v William Dowie Kidd, there had been a number of high profile, seemingly unjust convictions, including that of Derek Bentley, Ruth Ellis and Timothy Evans. The Homicide Act 1957 saw a partial reform of the definition surrounding murder, essentially dividing the crime of murder into two categories. Capital Murder – for example, the killing of a police officer or a child, multiple killings and murder involving a firearm – for which the death penalty would still apply; or murder, for which a life prison sentence would now apply. The Homicide Act also saw the introduction of the 'partial defence' doctrine, under which the defence might choose to seek clemency under such grounds as extreme provocation, a failed suicide pact or diminished responsibility (as opposed to insanity). The trial of William Kidd was just the fourth murder trial to take place in Scotland since the assent of the Homicide Act, but the first one in which the boundaries and definitions of this new legislation would be tested.

Coupled with William Kidd's use of chloroform, the tragic death of a child, and his attempt to use insanity as a defence, the trial promised to be one of the most controversial ever to be held at the High Court in Perth. The utilisation of chloroform in the crime of murder is an extremely rare occurrence – unlike in Hollywood movies. In fact, it was not technically a crime to administer chloroform to another human being. Nevertheless, the purchase of the drug was likely to attract attention in the 1950s.

Coincidentally, the rare use of chloroform as a tool of murder also features in my companion book, *Perthshire's Pound of Flesh*.

There was an intense atmosphere in the Perth courtroom as the trial of William Kidd finally opened on Tuesday, 20 October 1959. Lord Strachan presided, and began by warning the packed public gallery against any sudden outbursts of emotion.

After Douglas Reith QC entered William Kidd's defence of 'not guilty due to special grounds of insanity', the Crown, represented by the Advocate-Depute Mr James Law QC, began the case against the accused man. Later, in 1976, James Law would famously win the acquittal of Ian Waddell, on the charge of having murdered Rachel Ross in Ayr. However, in 1959, he was to be the advocate in charge of prosecuting William Kidd.

First to be called was William Kidd Junior, who recalled the events of 5 July, and of finding his mother's body under the bedclothes.

'William, please tell the court about your father's relationship with your mother and sister.'

'My father often quarrelled with my mother and sometimes he went away from home for fairly long periods. Recently he started taking my sister Christina with him.'

'Why?' James Law enquired.

'He was always annoyed when she spoke to boys,' the accused man's son explained, 'and on 3rd July he objected because she had gone to a dance and stayed the night with a friend.'

'How was your father's behaviour when you last saw him on the Saturday morning?'

'Before leaving the cottage on the morning of 4th July, I did notice that my father seemed a bit odd.'

'And did you know that he kept chemicals in the house?'

'My father was the tractor foreman on the farm, but he sometimes had to deal with the sheep too and I knew that he kept a bottle of ether in connection with his work.'

The evidence surrounding the presence of chloroform was pursued further by the prosecution, who then called James Rae, a chemist from Perth.

'Mr Rae, can you please tell the court what happened in the spring of 1959.'

'Yes. I received a telephone call from a man asking if he could purchase chloroform. It was rather an unusual request. I asked the man what he wanted it for. He said it was for the treatment of an animal, which I took to be a dog. I consulted my manager who agreed to the purchase providing that the man would call personally at the shop, which he did that afternoon. We supplied Mr Kidd with a form of chloroform used in liniments, but he came back a day or two later and asked for the proper anaesthetic chloroform as, he said, "it wasn't doing the job". So, we gave him a bottle of the anaesthetic type.'

The next witness, Samuel Smith, a farmhand from Strathmiglo who had previously worked with William Kidd, testified that:

'During the lambing season this year, Kidd inserted some stitches into a ewe and it was giving some trouble. He put a pad with either ether or chloroform on It over the ewe's nostrils, and he held there for two three minutes. The ewe quietened down then.'

Evidence against William Kidd appeared to be mounting, would the forensic testimony help or hinder the defence's case?

9 – THE DOUBLE CHLOROFORM MURDER
(Part Two)

The courtroom waited in hushed expectation as Dr Edgar Rentoul, the senior lecturer in Forensic Medicine at Glasgow University, was called to the witness stand. Dr Rentoul was much respected and appeared as an expert medical witness in many of Scotland's most famous murder trials of the post-war era.

'When we removed the bedclothes, which had been placed on top of the victim, we observed that her hands had been tied in front of her, the cord then looped round her body, and run down to her ankles, which were also tied together,' Rentoul began.

Before continuing, Dr Rentoul displayed a cardboard model of the victim's wrists and ankles to illustrate exactly how Mrs Kidd had been bound:

'I examined both Mrs Kidd's body and that of her daughter Christina and formed the opinion that both had died from suffocation and that chloroform had been administered to them shortly before death. Both had been suffocated with another object, most likely a pillowcase. In both cases, death had occurred about midnight on July 4th. I have no doubt that the cord on Mrs Kidd's wrist had been placed there after death.'

'Thank you, Dr Rentoul. No further questions.'

Following the completion of the forensic evidence, the key question of William Kidd's sanity at the time of the murders was next to be explored. Dr David Ross, the consultant psychiatrist from Stratheden Hospital in Cupar (the former Fife and Kinross District Asylum), had kept William Kidd under observation since his incarceration:

'I twice examined Mr Kidd,' Dr Ross explained, 'and found no evidence that he is, or had been insane. He did not give me any clear picture of the exact time his wife and daughter died. During my discussions with him, he was able to remember only to the point at which he was arguing with his wife in the presence of his daughter. His next recollection was "coming to" in a café on the other side of the Forth, some time later.'

'And do you consider, Dr Ross, that Mr Kidd is suffering from hysterical amnesia?'

'I have my doubts whether he is experiencing any form of amnesia at all. If he is, in fact, suffering from hysterical amnesia following the events of that weekend, that is, in my opinion, not a form of mental illness, but a condition which consists wholly of a failure to remember.'

'Thank you, Dr Ross.'

With that assessment, James Law QC rested and Douglas Reith stood up to begin the case for the defence. In an attempt to limit the damage inflicted by Dr Ross, Reith immediately recalled the consultant psychiatrist to the witness box:

'Dr Ross,' the defence advocate began, 'I want you to assume that Kidd killed his wife and daughter after a late-night quarrel concerning his daughter's friendship with a middle-aged bus driver. I also want you to assume that the accused man left his wife's body in the house, propped his daughter's body in the front passenger seat of his car and then drove through Fife, stopping to speak to several people on the way, and even stopping to buy petrol. After disposing of the body in a copse, he then stopped his car soon afterwards to give a stranger a lift. Would these have been the actions of a normal man, Doctor?'

Dr Ross shook his head and admitted, 'No, they would have been unusual and very odd.'

'Thank you, Doctor.'

Reith then produced William Kidd's Army records and read several detailed passages to the jury:

'Mr Kidd was sent home from Africa in 1944 and discharged because he suffered from hysterical amnesia, details of which are listed here in his Army medical file. The records refer to Mr Kidd's history of suffering from periodic blackouts, during which times he performed actions which he could not subsequently recall.'

Mrs Mary Steedman, from Glenfoot, Abernethy, was then asked to testify on behalf of the defendant:

'I have known William Kidd since he was a little boy and always regarded him as a brother. He suffered head injuries twice in childhood and he had started wandering away from home even at an early age. In later years he often went away for weeks at a time. Since his daughter, Christina, was about twelve years old he has been very worried about her association with a bus driver. He has even shown me letters which the girl had received from that man. He was about fifty, and Christina is only fourteen now, but she looks and acts older.'

It was now time for the accused man to stand in the dock and speak on his own behalf. Kidd would face an examination lasting 70 minutes, to which the jury of nine men and six women listened intently.

'I felt something come over me,' Kidd began, 'during a quarrel in the cottage on that Saturday night. After that, I have no recollection of what happened until the next day, when I found myself in the car, miles from home, and driving towards England. I did not learn that my wife and daughter were dead until July 7th when the police detained me while I was working in a fruit field at Worcester.'

'And has this kind of thing happened to you before?'

'I've been in the habit of wandering away from home for no apparent reason since I sustained a head injury in the Army.

I was discharged in 1944.'

'Do you know why you were discharged?'

'I understood it was because of mental illness.'

'Thank you, Mr Kidd. Could you please now tell the court about the arguments with your daughter.'

'Since Christina was about twelve I have been worried about her behaviour with the opposite sex. Not only boys of her own age, but with much older persons. I believed she was having improper relations with them. I spoke to her about it, and we had lots of quarrels.'

'And what part did your wife play in this, Mr Kidd?'

'She always took the girl's side, and always said that the things I'd been worrying about weren't happening.'

'Thank you. Please continue.'

'For the past eighteen months I had been particularly worried about my daughter's friendship with a 50-year-old bus driver, a married man called Duncan Stuart of Dunblane. Latterly, my worry about Christina and Stuart has increased, and I'd quarrelled more about it with my wife. But, despite this, we had a pleasant evening on July 4th. Me and my wife went for a walk and returned home at 9pm to watch TV. I had two bottles of stout and a small sherry. My daughter returned home about 11.15pm and a quarrel started when I mentioned Stuart's name. Tempers heated up, but I can't remember how the argument ended. I have a hazy recollection of my wife and daughter leaving the living room, but I remember nothing further until Sunday. The next thing I remember was giving someone a lift in the car near Grangemouth. He was travelling south.'

'Thank you, Mr Kidd. And what happened after your final quarrel? Did your temper get the better of you?'

'No. My temper didn't get the better of me. Something just came over me. I felt the blood going to my head, and I remember nothing else until the next day.

The defence's final witness was then called to the stand. Dr Matthew Devlin, the Deputy Physician Superintendent of Bellside Mental Hospital in Larbert, testified that:

'During my examination of the accused, I came to the conclusion that he was suffering from hysterical amnesia and genuinely could not recall events which occurred in his home after midnight on July 4th.'

'Thank you, Dr Devlin. And do you believe that Mr Kidd was responsible for his actions during that night?'

Dr Devlin considered his answer for a moment, before answering:

'There are two possibilities. One was that he became so incensed during the quarrel that he carried out the deeds in anger. The more likely possibility, however, which is in keeping with his medical history, was that under great emotional stress he went into an abnormal state of reduced awareness.'

With the case for the defence now concluded, Douglas Reith QC began his summation, which contained one or two remarkable things – a memorable phrase, designed to remain in the jury's mind and to provide newspaper editors with a catchy headline, and an extraordinary revelation which would surely now be struck from the record had it been attempted in a modern trial.

'Ladies and gentlemen of the jury, I have been placed at a considerable disadvantage in putting forward the accused's defence, because of his amnesia and inability to give any legal instruction regarding the vital period of time in this case. With regard to whether he was responsible for his actions during this period of forgetfulness, I refer you, members of the jury, to my client's obsession over his daughter's conduct with members of the opposite sex. However, the post-mortem medical examination of his daughter showed that she was not a virgin and his fears had been justified.

Even if we ignore the medical testimony, or the accused man's history, his fantastic behaviour clearly shows that here we have a man who is as mad as a hatter. I ask you, the jury, to find the accused insane at the time of the alleged crime, or failing that, to find that he was of diminished responsibility. The latter finding would have the effect of reducing the charges from murder to culpable homicide. I would humbly suggest that the sentence to impose on this man should bear these factors in mind.'

It only remained for Lord Strachan to sum up the complicated legal aspects of the case for the jury, before dismissing them to consider their verdict:

'Members of the jury, this case has been unusual both in respect of the means by which it was alleged the victims were killed, and in respect of the special defence of insanity at the time of the alleged acts. Please remember, that it is not claimed that William Kidd is now insane, but only that he was at the time.

The first thing I want to say to you is that, in this case, the death sentence is not involved. By a comparatively recent statute Parliament has now made distinctions between types of murder. Certain types of murder were classified as capital murder, and it is only in capital murders that the death sentence is now pronounced. This is not a capital murder. You, of course, are not really concerned with any question of sentence; that is entirely a matter for me, but in view of the recent change in the law, and in case you might be under any misunderstanding, I thought it preferable to make that point clear at the outset.

The first question you must ask yourself is this – has the Crown proved beyond reasonable doubt that the accused committed the acts with which he is charged under one or other, or both, of the charges in the indictment?

It is certainly a strange story. On Kidd's drive through Fife, with his daughter's body propped up beside him, you may ask whether he would have done that if someone else had killed her. It must be said that there is not much evidence to connect Kidd with the death of his wife, however, you may think the same hand killed both.

In relation to the special defence of insanity, here the burden of proof lies on the accused and his defence advocate. If you hold that his loss of memory was genuine, it may be that he can't remember some of the pieces of evidence which have been put before you at this trial, and which may have even tended to strengthen his proof of insanity. You must give full allowance for that possibility when considering whether it was probable that the accused was insane at the time of the alleged crimes.

You may also wish to consider that Kidd was only pretending to have suffered from a loss of memory, and it should be said that this would provide a very useful protection against cross-examination in the witness box.

Regarding his conduct after the deaths, all of the doctors agreed that it had been odd, to say the least. He tied up his wife apparently after death, and then took his daughter in the front seat of his car, although she was already dead. If he knew she was dead, it was certainly very odd conduct to drive across Fife and talk to people on the way with the body on view beside him. Is it a possible explanation that he thought she was only anaesthetised? That is for the jury to decide. However, he then disposed of the body by hiding it in a copse. Was it possible that he then realised that she was not anaesthetised but dead?

Members of the jury, there is no such verdict as "Guilty but insane". That is entirely illogical. If you decide that he committed the acts but was insane, your verdict should be acquittal on the grounds of insanity. There are five possible verdicts: not guilty; not proven; a verdict that he committed the act or acts, but was insane at the time – which must mean an acquittal on the grounds of insanity; guilty of culpable homicide; or, finally, guilty of murder as libelled.'

The jury were then dismissed to consider their verdict and William Kidd was taken back to his cell to await his fate.

After precisely 60 minutes the jury returned to the hushed courtroom. Asked if they had reached a verdict, the foreman responded in the affirmative, 'Yes, your honour, we find the defendant guilty of culpable homicide.'

'Was your verdict a unanimous one?'

'Yes, your honour.'

Lord Strachan thanked the jury for their dedication during

the intense three-day trial, before then turning to William Kidd, who stood ashen faced in the dock:

'Prisoner at the bar, the jury has found you guilty of the dastardly acts with which you have been charged, but has seen fit to reduce the quality of the crimes from murder to that of culpable homicide. Nonetheless, they were very serious crimes indeed. It is the sentence of this court that you will be sent to prison for fifteen years.'

Unlike his historic namesake 250 years earlier – the notorious Captain William Kidd from nearby Dundee – William Dowie Kidd escaped the hangman's noose, largely thanks to the recent changes in the law and the liberal sensibilities of this 1959 Sottish jury. Even though the jurors clearly did not believe Kidd's claim of insanity, they chose to believe that there was no intent to kill. Despite purchasing chloroform three months prior to the killings, which appears to demonstrate premeditation, disabling his victims before killing them, then tying up one body, and disposing of the other, the jury opted for a verdict of culpable homicide, which is defined under Scottish Law as a crime:

'Where the accused has caused loss of life through wrongful conduct but where there was no intention to kill or wicked recklessness.'

There have been many defendants convicted of murder on far less compelling evidence.

Following the tragic events of 1959, the three remaining children were left to rebuild their lives without their mother, while their father was removed to begin his incarceration. After serving the majority of his sentence, Kidd was released and relocated to a small village near Cambridge, where he found employment on a farm, never troubling the police again. He spent his final years quietly, working and spending his spare time gardening and entering his prize vegetables in competitions at local agricultural shows. He eventually passed away in 1996 at the age of 72, his new neighbours blissfully unaware of his past transgressions.

10 – THE PHANTOM RASPBERRY BLOWER

June 1938 – Those of a certain age might remember a regular 1970s television sketch by *The Two Ronnies* entitled 'The Phantom Raspberry Blower of Old London Town', in which the sound of someone blowing a raspberry inevitably led to a gruesome murder. Comic, yes, but hardly credible as a motive for murder. Or so you might think. Surprisingly, this strange and surreal chain of events played out on the streets of Perth in 1938.

Late in the evening on Saturday, 25 June 1938, Alexander Dingwall and his partner, Catherine Duff, left a dance in Perth City centre and began to stroll home along West Mill Street, towards his lodgings in Inchaffray Street. It was a warm and still summer night. As they reached the bottom of the street, however, the stillness was disturbed by the sound of two men arguing. As the couple walked past the two men, they distinctly heard one threaten the other with the words, 'I'll knock your bloody head off!'

They hurried on, but a few moments later the two men ran past them, one chasing the other. Alexander Dingwall would later describe the events that followed to the police:

'Just at the top of the incline at the Ladeside, the second man appeared to pounce on the first and there was a thud as the first man fell. The second man then left the scene and came walking past Catherine and me.

The first man was left lying stretched out on his back. I approached him and he was groaning a lot. Another man came from the other direction and we carried the poor man down to Baker's Buildings. I then saw the second man again. He was stood in the shadows at Mill Close. I couldn't make out who he was, but he had blue overalls on. I turned round but when I looked again, he was gone.'

Sadly, the man on the ground, David Neil, a 33-year-old

painter with a wife and daughter, was so severely injured that he died at approximately midnight close to the City Mills. By 8am the following morning a murder enquiry was officially launched.

Unfortunately, the witness, Alexander Dingwall was only able to inform the police that the man he had seen the previous night was 'young and dressed in blue overalls.' It was a sparse and sketchy description, but it did remind Inspector Alistair McInnes, a quick-thinking Perth police officer, that he had often noticed someone in blue overalls walking backwards and forward to work along Barrack Street. However, he had only seen the man at a distance and was not sure if he would recognise him again. Nevertheless, he decided to take a chance. By Sunday lunchtime, only twelve hours after the attack on David Neil, Inspector McInnes was in Barrack Street. The only solution, he decided, would be to knock on the door of every house in the street until he either located the man or found someone who recognised the vague description.

Inspector McInnes decided on a systematic approach and started at the St Ninian's end of the road. He made a careful note of the time as he tapped on the first door:

'12.20pm. 18 Barrack Street.'

A young man answered the door and, noticing the police officer's uniform, said, 'Oh, come in, I was just coming to the police station to see you. I did not mean to kill him.'

Inspector McInnes was taken aback, but remembering his duty as a police officer, began to advise the man, 'Say nothing more, as a murder charge is likely to be preferred against you...' However, before he could finish, the young man blurted out:

'I'm James Sullivan. Last night, another fellow with a mouth organ, and I, were having a singsong when David Neil passed by and gave us the "raspberry". I did not mean to kill him.'

By 12.22pm Inspector McInnes had located the murderer and apparently solved the crime. James Sullivan was taken to Perth City Police Station to await his arraignment the following morning.

By the time Monday arrived, news of James Sullivan's arrest had already swept around the Fair City. It transpired that the detained man was something of a local celebrity. Sullivan had played as a junior for Newburgh Tayside Football Club in 1927, and for Perth St Leonard's until 1931. A footballer of not inconsiderable talent, he had been awarded trials for Dundee United and Alloa, and was a minor local celebrity, particularly in the world of local football. Sullivan may well have known the victim, David Neil, through their respective interest in sport. David Neil was a cousin of John Smeaton, a well-known professional footballer, who had previously played for St Johnstone, Blackburn, and Sunderland, and a keen golfer like John Sullivan.

On Monday, 27 June, Sullivan was taken to Perth Sheriff's Court, and placed in front of Mr Harry Douglas, the Clerk of the Court, who read the charge to him:

'James Sullivan, you are charged that you did, about 11.45pm on 25th June, 1938, on the path at the Ladeside in the Burgh of Perth, about fifteen yards or thereby north of the north wall of the City Mill, assault David Neil, coach painter, of 1b Hunter Terrace, Perth, by striking him with your fist and knocking him to the ground whereby he was so severely injured that he died, and you did thus murder him.'

Sullivan was not asked to plead, but was taken downstairs and removed to Perth Prison in a police car. Instructions were then issued to Professor Sydney Smith from Edinburgh University, and Dr Moffat from Perth Royal Infirmary to carry out a post-mortem examination of the body. A trial date was set for Tuesday, 15 November at the High Court in Perth.

A month after the death of David Neil, a display of James Sullivan's popularity and standing in the local community was demonstrated at the accused man's bail hearing. Unusually, for a crime of such severity, Sullivan was granted bail to the amount of £50 (today's equivalent of approximately £4,500). Sheriff Valentine expressed some concern; not regarding the release of a possibly violent offender, but over the sum involved:

'While I know nothing of the circumstances of the case,' the Sheriff explained, 'it seems to me that the suggested sum of £50, made by the solicitor, is rather a big one for a brewery worker to pay.'

Sheriff Valentine was reassured that Sullivan could raise the money with the assistance of friends and with the support of his employer, John Wright & Co Ltd, the Perth-based bottling company. The manager director of the firm, Robert Nimmo, spoke out on Sullivan's behalf. Conveniently for Sullivan, Robert Nimmo was also Lord Provost of Perth.

James Sullivan's trial commenced on 15 November at the High Court with a jury of twelve men and three women. Sheriff Valentine presided over the events, with Robert Milligan KC appearing for the Crown. Robert Milligan would later become Lord President of Scotland and an elected member of Parliament. Although it is doubtful that he would ever again become entangled in quite such a bizarre case. Norman Hunter from McCash & Hunter Solicitors represented James Sullivan.

The prosecution began their case with a poignant appearance by Jane Neil, the widow of the murdered man:

'I last saw my husband alive at 1pm on Saturday 25th June,'

she explained to the court, 'He was in the habit of playing golf on the North Inch course with the Perth Artisans Club. The next time I saw him was in the middle of the night when I was asked to attend Perth Royal Infirmary to identify his body.'

She was led in tears from the witness stand; a sight which clearly touched the heart of even the most dispassionate juror. With Alexander Dingwall, the eyewitness who had heard Sullivan and Neil arguing, next to testify, Hunter realised how decisive his cross-examination would need to be.

Alexander Dingwall once again described the events of 25th June:

'One of them said "I'll knock your bloody head off." After they ran past us, the second man pounced on the first man. There was a thud as the first man fell. The second man then left the scene.'

'Tell me, Mr Dingwall,' began Hunter, in his cross-examination for the defence, 'Do you know which of the two men passed that remark?'

'No. I do not know.' Dingwall conceded.

'It was dark then?'

'Yes.'

'And you were not close?'

'We were a little way away, yes.'

'And if I suggest to you, Mr Dingwall, that the first man turned round, and faced the second man, would that be the case?'

'No.' replied the witness.

Hunter continued probing, 'If he had turned round, you perhaps would not have seen that in the dark?'

'No, I might not have I suppose.'

'May it not have been the case that when the first man turned round, the second man accidentally bumped into him?'

'I do not know.'

'You were not in a position to see all that was happening, then?'

'That is correct.'

'Was there a struggle between the two men, then?'

'No. I did not see one.'

Hunter could afford a smile. He had clearly created some doubt in the chain of events leading to David Neil's murder. However, the next person to testify, James Hutchinson (the witness who had helped Alexander Dingwall pick up Mr Neil from the floor on the night of his death), had approached the scene from the opposite side, and had a very different view of the events:

'I was coming down Ladeside from the Crieff Road direction when I saw a man walking towards me and there was another fellow running behind him. The first man turned round and the fellow who was running behind him caught up and struck him with his fist several times on the face. The first man put up his hands to protect himself, but he didn't attempt to strike a blow. Then he fell on his back.'

Hunter again desperately attempted to limit the damage in his cross-examination of the witness, 'May it have been that the second man accidentally collided with the first man, knocking him over?'

'No.'

'Was the man who fell over perhaps drunk.'

'No, I don't think so.'

There was some light relief next, when Inspector McInnes explained his extraordinary fortune in locating the suspect so easily. The story of the 'raspberry' noise alleged made by David Neil caused much amusement in the public gallery, especially when Sheriff Valentine was forced to ask the witness, 'What on earth is a "raspberry", Inspector?'

'It is a rather vulgar noise made by the mouth, your honour.'

The trial soon returned to more serious matters when Professor Sydney Smith detailed the post-mortem findings to the court:

'The injuries on the back of the head could have been caused by a man falling heavily on the back of his head onto a hard surface, but it would be very difficult for all the bruises on his body to have been caused by a fall. There was an injury at the back of the head, one in the small of the back, one on the forearm, and a small haemorrhage on the epi-cranium. Some of these injuries might have been caused by a blow, and I am of the opinion that there had been some outside influence.

I also completed an analysis of the stomach contents which showed 1.2% of alcohol.'

After some discussion over how much alcohol David Neil had consumed during the day, in which a witness from the golf tournament suggested that the victim had 'drunk two lagers and a nip of whisky', the prosecution rested its case. It was now time for Norman Hunter to present the defence.

Firstly, several character witnesses were produced who all testified to James Sullivan's good nature and placid disposition. Canon McDaniel from St John's Roman Catholic Church told the court that, 'Mr Sullivan has been a member of my flock for the eighteen years I have been in Perth. I cannot imagine the accused man deliberately attacking and injuring anyone. He was a popular fellow.'

John Bissett, a work colleague of Sullivan's, told the jury that 'he was a good-natured fellow you could trust' and Lord Provost Nimmo again testified on the defendant's behalf.

Then came the most dramatic development of the trial so far. The accused man, James Sullivan, entered the witness box. He spoke openly and at length to the court,

'I am thirty-one years of age and a brewer's bottler at John Wright & Co in Perth. I have been there for thirteen years. I am a married man with three children. I have been in the habit of assisting in a local bar on Saturdays, and on the night in question I left these premises between ten-thirty and eleven. I went up to a club in South Methven Street to see some of my chums, and I stayed there until about 11.10pm, when I started off for home. On the way, in Mill Wynd, I met John Jenkins and his son in a doorway, playing his mouth organ and singing. I'm a bit of a singer, I've sung at some concerts.

A fellow walking past looked in and he said something

about me not being able to sing – and then he gave me the "raspberry".'

'Did this fellow appear to you to have had some drink?' enquired Mr Hunter.

'Yes.'

'And in what manner did he give you the raspberry and make his remarks?'

'He made the remarks aggressively. I went outside to demand an explanation, and the man said more objectionable words and then raced off. He went off in the direction of the Ladeside, and I went after him for an explanation and apology. I caught up with him, and then he sort of turned round and stumbled and I was running and I accidentally fell over him. He fell on his back.'

'Did you strike him any blow, or even attempt to strike any blow?'

'No.'

'Did you put up your own hands to save yourself from falling?'

'Yes. Then I walked away, not wishing to be involved in a breach of the peace. Then I went home. The next thing I knew about the matter was on Sunday morning, when I heard people speaking about a tragedy, but I did not immediately link myself with it. Later that morning, when I found out where it had occurred, I thought I might be connected. I was just preparing to go to the police station when a detective came to my door.'

'Did you say you would knock his bloody head off?' asked the defence counsel.

'No, I did not.'

'Did you feel like knocking his head off?'

'No.'

Despite a spirited attempt by the prosecution to cross-examine James Sullivan's testimony, the defendant did not deviate from his version of events. The tide in the trial seemed to be swinging in favour of the accused man.

Hunter then introduced his master stroke – the defence's

own forensic specialist, Professor D F Chappell from Dundee Royal Infirmary. From the outset of the investigation James Sullivan's advocate had requested that his own medical expert be permitted to examine David Neil's body. Professor Chappell explained the difficulty to the court:

'On Sunday 26th June I tried to gain admission to the post-mortem examination but was not permitted.'

'What did you think at the time, Professor?'

'That it was highly important for the accused to be represented at that examination.'

'And what were your findings when you were finally given access?'

'I carried out an examination of the deceased on Monday. At that time the skull was open and the brain had been removed during the earlier post-mortem. This made it difficult for me to make a satisfactory examination.'

'And what were your conclusions, Professor?'

'There were no bruises on the face and body and several parts of the deceased's skull were unusually thin; but it was not fractured.'

'But', Hunter asked, 'if the deceased had been assaulted on the face and body by an assailant, should there have been bruises?'

'Yes, but there were none present.'

'And, in your opinion, Professor Chappell, what caused the injuries to the deceased?'

'In my opinion the injuries are consistent with a heavy fall, although I cannot exclude that certain of injuries may have been caused by a fist.'

'Thank you, Professor.'

The unsatisfactory post-mortem evidence seemed to be enough for Sherriff Valentine. He called Milligan to the bench, and the prosecution agreed to the charge of murder being dropped. The jurors were then instructed to consider a charge of culpable homicide against James Sullivan, which was defined for them:

'Culpable homicide is committed when the accused person has caused loss of life through wrongful conduct but where there was no intention to kill or wicked recklessness.'

The jury then retired to consider their verdict. Although no longer facing a charge of murder – and potentially the death penalty – culpable homicide could still carry a life sentence, should the judge deem the offence serious enough. James Sullivan's fate still hung in the balance. However, he would not have to wait long to discover the outcome.

Thirty minutes later, the jury returned. There was a breathless silence as the Clerk of the Court, A P Oliver, addressed the foreman,

'Have you arrived at a verdict?'

'We find the panel not guilty,' replied the foreman.

Asked if it was a unanimous decision, he answered, 'By a majority.'

The public gallery burst into spontaneous applause and Sheriff Valentine formally dismissed James Sullivan. Perhaps the only murder trial in history, in which the blowing of a raspberry could be considered the motive, was over. James Sullivan left the court a free man. He remained in Perth for the rest of his life, and did not trouble the police again. He passed away in Bridge of Earn Hospital in 1969, aged 62.

There may have been an early clue into the unsatisfactory and inconclusive nature of the post-mortem. David Neil had been buried with unseemly haste, in a private ceremony at Wellshill Cemetery, Perth – just three days after his tragic death. Members of the public were banned from attending his funeral by an entourage of plain-clothed police officers who blocked the cemetery entrance.

11 – 'I WOKE UP AND FOUND HER DEAD'
(Part One)

September 1947 – Archibald Wood was employed as a porter and signalman at Justinhaugh Railway Station, on the Forfar and Brechin Railway. Early on the morning of Friday, 12 September 1947, he reported the death of his wife to the police. After first leaving the couple's three young children with a neighbour, Wood hurried to the local police station in Forfar, three miles away.

An anxious and flustered Wood explained to the police constable on duty, 'I woke up at seven this morning and found her dead.' Both he and his wife were 27 years of age.

Following his statement, two police officers, accompanied by the local doctor, visited the Wood's home at Railway Cottages in the hamlet of Justinhaugh. Due to the sudden and unexpected nature of the death, coupled with the deceased lady's young age, an immediate post-mortem was ordered. The body of Isabella Wood was then removed to Stracathro Hospital to await the arrival of Scotland's two leading forensic medical experts of the era, Professor Glaister, the pathologist from the University of Glasgow, and Dr Imrie, the Glasgow Police surgeon. Working together, the two men concluded that Isabella had 'died by unnatural means.' Word was then sent to the police in Forfar. The small and normally peaceful hamlet of Justinhaugh then became a flurry of activity, as officers swopped to arrest Archibald Wood for the alleged murder of his wife. Wood seemed both shocked and disturbed as he was driven away in a waiting police car.

A protracted period of questioning and evidence gathering began until, finally, Wood was given an arraignment hearing (known as a pleading diet in Scotland) at the High Court in Perth. Looking tired and dishevelled and dressed in a blue raincoat and pin-striped trousers, he was charged:

'Archibald Wood, you are charged, that you did, on either September 12th or 13th this year, in your house at Station Cottages, Justinhaugh, assault Isabella Taylor Campbell, or Wood, by striking her on the face, seizing and compressing her by the throat, and that you did murder her contrary to common law. And that you did previously evince malice towards her by repeatedly beating and assaulting her and threatening to strangle her. How do you plead?'

Unusually for the High Court at Perth, this was the second murder charge of that morning's diet. The previous defendant had entered a long and complicated defence of insanity. In marked contrast, Archibald Wood's entire appearance that morning lasted less than one minute. Through his solicitor, G A Craig from Forfar, he entered a plea of 'not guilty', and promptly left the courthouse under guard.

In the meantime, Isabella Wood was buried in a quiet family ceremony at the parish church in Liff, a small village three miles from Dundee and around fifteen miles away from Justinhaugh.

A trial date was set for Tuesday, 16 December 1947 and it was announced that nine items of evidence would be presented and 27 witnesses produced. A jury of ten men and just five women was selected, a ratio which some commentators felt might favour the accused man. Archibald Wood took his place in the dock, this time appearing well-groomed in a grey pin-striped suit and dark tie. He seemed quietly confident. Wood was represented in court by John Cameron, KC, while the Crown's case was conducted by Sinclair Shaw, the Advocate-Depute for Perthshire. Lord Carmont presided from the bench (a judge who would soon gain a fearsome reputation for tough sentencing as he dealt with the so-called 'Razor Gangs' in Glasgow, resulting in the phrase 'Doing a Carmont' entering the legal lexicon).

David Reid, a neighbour of the Woods, was called as the first witness:

'I am a railway ganger,' explained Mr Reid, 'Wood and his

wife have been our neighbours at Justinhaugh for about four years. On September 12th I went to bed about 10 o'clock and nothing unusual happened during the night. I rose at 5.30am, as usual, and went to the door and took in the newspapers. About 6.55am, as I was leaving for work, I saw Wood coming from his house with his hand on his head. He laid his head against a drainer that stood outside the back door, which they used to set a basin on, for their pots and pans. I thought he looked funny, so I asked him what was wrong. He told me that he'd found his wife dead in bed. He also said, "she might have fallen, as she was all black and blue about the jaw." I then rushed into my house and told the wife. When I came back outside Wood was still there. I then went out to work to phone the doctor. Wood was still standing in the same position when I left.'

David Reid's wife, Ann, was next to testify:

'Mrs Wood and me were on friendly terms. She told me on more than one occasion that her husband knocked her around and had tried to strangle her. They were not a happy couple. One evening in April or May when it was raining, Mrs Wood passed our window and she did not have a coat on. Next day, when I asked why she was out without her coat, she said to me, "It was that stupid bastard. He tried to choke me last night.

I just ran out." Another time I said to her that she would do better to see a doctor, or else, as it was about time something was done.'

'And what did you mean exactly by that remark, Mrs Reid?' enquired the Advocate-Depute.

'I meant that I was going to be getting up some morning and find Mrs Wood lying dead. During the course of this year, I've many a time heard shouts coming from the Wood's house – and it was more or less always Mrs Wood screaming. I've heard Mr Wood shouting and on more than one occasion I heard him say he would murder her.'

'Thank you, Mrs Reid. Moving on to the morning of the tragedy, what did you see?'

'When I saw Mr Wood on the morning of his wife's death, I had the feeling he was fatigued from want of sleep. I made him a cup of tea.'

It was now time for the defence to cross-examine Mrs Reid, and John Cameron KC leapt on the witness's last remark:

'What did you mean, Mrs Reid, when you said you "had the feeling he was fatigued"?'

'Well, he just looked tired, I meant.'

'Really? Doubtless any one of us might looked "fatigued" – as you have put it – at such an early hour and upon finding our spouse deceased next to us. However, moving on. If you really felt that Mr Wood might murder his wife at any moment, why did you not inform the authorities earlier?'

'Well, I did not feel it was my place.'

'That is understandable, none of us would wish to take such formal steps. Why, then, did you only ever interfere personally with one dispute between the couple?'

'Well, it's not my place and, besides, Mrs Wood was not a very good housewife or mother to the three bairns, and their arguments got worse. She seemed to have no heart left for it all,' Mrs Reid replied.

John Cameron continued:

'Tell me, Mrs Reid, I put it to you that your story is entirely made up, and that you did not like Archibald Wood.'

'I had nothing against him until he lifted his hands to her.'

'And yet you have raked up all the gossip in the neighbourhood, that you could think of, now that this man is on trial for his life?'

'I have only told you, sir, what his wife told me, and what I have seen for myself.'

'And, Mrs Reid, I take it you do not believe the accused man's statement that he had wakened up and found his wife dead in bed next to him?'

'No sir,' Mrs Reid replied defiantly, 'I do not think a man would have taken time to dress himself if he woke up and found his wife lying dead next to him, even to the point of lacing his boots. After the bruised faces he had given her, he was fit for anything.'

'Fit even for murder?'

'Yes,' Mrs Reid replied emphatically.

'Very well. No further questions.'

Although the defence advocate may have thought he had somewhat nullified the potentially detrimental effect of Mrs Reid's testimony, the evidence of the next witness appeared to be much more damaging to his client's case.

Mr Francis Stevenson MacLeod, the stationmaster at Justinhaugh, recalled an incident from earlier in the year, 'In May or June of this year, Archibald Wood was in my office at the Station House, when his wife, Mrs Wood, came in. She had a discoloured left eye. She asked me to call the police and said, "I am going to put an end to this." Her husband then lifted his right hand, as if to strike her, and said, "Do you want another one?" I put a stop to it and advised her to go into the other room and use the telephone if she wanted to.'

'And what had the Woods been quarrelling about?' enquired the prosecution.

'It was about cigarettes. Any time I asked Mrs Wood why she was upset it was always about cigarettes. It was common knowledge that they argued a lot.'

The next witness, Constable David Neilson from Tanna-dice, testified to finding, 'the dead woman lying fully clothed underneath the covers on the bed. I saw bruise marks under her chin which extended to the left ear. There was also a number of scratches on the throat. I asked Wood if he had any explanation to offer for this and, without being cautioned, the accused man said this to me (the constable removed his notebook from his pocket and recited Archibald Wood's statement verbatim) "I came home last night about ten o'clock and found my wife reading in the chair. She had the supper ready and we took it together. After supper I gave her a cigarette and left her reading in the chair by the fire. One of the children was still awake and I thought she would stay up until the child went to sleep. So, I went to bed at 10.15 and I did not hear her coming to bed, but I am a sound sleeper. I wakened about six and felt her hand which was cold. I tried to waken her, but found that she was dead. I then examined her and I found a mark on her chin which I swear was not there when I went to bed. She has been taking dizzy turns for some time, and I think she had fallen against the chair."'

'Thank you, Constable. And what did you do after you had finished noting down the accused man's statement?'

Constable Neilson carefully replaced his notebook back in the breast pocket of his tunic, before continuing his evidence:

'I also found other bruises at the back of Mrs Wood's left ear and some scratches on her forehead. In the house itself there was no sign of a struggle having taken place. On the table were the remains of a meal, and the book which Mrs Wood had been reading was lying open on the chair. Two of the children were sleeping in the same room. The other child was asleep in the other room. They did not seem to have been disturbed by all the goings on.'

'Thank you, Constable Neilson, that is all.'

Dr David Myles, the family's doctor from Forfar, entered the witness box next:

'I have attended the family since 1943. However, when I last saw the deceased she was in poor health and very anaemic. She was poorly nourished and somewhat shaky on her feet.'

'Thank you, Doctor. And would you explain for the court exactly what happened when you were called to Station Cottages on the day of Mrs Wood's death?'

'When I made a superficial examination of the body, I found slight superficial abrasions on both sides of the neck. My examination was about 10.40am, and I estimated that death had occurred about ten hours previously, probably between midnight and 1am. I could not find sufficient evidence of the cause of death and refused to issue a statutory certificate at that time.'

Again, Mr Cameron KC for the defence, cross-examined the witness:

'Tell me, Dr Myles, in what condition did you find the house?'

'I found the Woods' home very untidy. In fact, during the whole time I have been their family doctor, it was always in that state.'

'Thank you, Doctor,' continued Mr Cameron, 'was it possible, then, that Mrs Wood fell, or perhaps tripped, due to the untidy state of the house? What opinion did you form?'

'I did not immediately assume that Mrs Wood had fallen, but I also did not immediately draw the opinion that the cause of death had been strangulation by manual throttling. Nevertheless, I was concerned that something abnormal had occurred.'

'Abnormal?'

'Yes. I advised the police in Forfar that a post-mortem would be necessary in this case. Returning to the deceased's condition' the doctor continued, 'it was possible that her anaemic state may have caused her to suffer from dizzy turns and fainting fits. Her pregnancy might also have been a factor which caused dizziness...'

'Mrs Wood was pregnant?' interrupted Mr Cameron,

'That does add another complication to the medical evidence.' The defence counsel's comment appeared to be a statement rather than a question, and was clearly intended for the benefit of the fifteen jurors, rather than in response to the doctor's revelation. 'Please continue, Doctor Myles.'

'As I was saying, there are many other causes for dizziness which could have been anaemia and a lack of reasonable nourishment.'

'Thank you, Doctor,' continued the defence advocate, 'and did you examine the spring mattress from the bedroom at Station Cottages?'

The mattress was produced in court as the first exhibit in the trial.

'Yes, I did,' responded Dr Myles.

'And would you agree, Doctor, that the chains and springs are quite rough edged and in such a condition, that any collision with such rough edges might very well produce scratches or abrasions on the neck?

'Yes, that is certainly possible.' agreed Dr Myles.

'Thank you, Doctor. No further questions.'

Next came the pivotal forensic evidence in the case which, the jurors were warned, would include one particularly gruesome exhibit. Professor John Glaister from the Forensic Medicine Department at Glasgow University, who had performed the post-mortem on the instruction of the Forfar Police, was summoned to the stand. Professor Glaister had testified in many high-profile cases during a long and distinguished career. Nevertheless, it is unlikely that he was prepared for the reception awaiting him in the Perth courtroom on that December day. In total, his appearance would last four hours and involve a heated exchange with the defence counsel.

First, however, came the prosecution's carefully prepared examination of Professor Glaister and the production of one vital and macabre piece of evidence, extracted during the post-mortem.

12 – 'I WOKE UP AND FOUND HER DEAD'
(Part Two)

Professor John Glaister began his evidence by testifying that:

'It is my opinion that death in this case resulted from the effects of a compression of the tissues in the victim's neck.'

'And could you give an approximate time at which death took place, Professor Glaister?' enquired Sinclair Shaw for the Crown.

'I am of the opinion that Mrs Wood died three to four hours after a meal had been digested. If the meal had been taken at ten o'clock, death would have, occurred in the neighbourhood of one-thirty to two o'clock. The injuries were consistent with the assailant's right hand having been applied to the victim's neck.'

'If this sort of attack was done through a quick, violent grasp, Professor, how long would it take for a person who was grasped in that manner to become unconscious?'

'That very much depends on the varying circumstances.' replied the Professor.

'And, Professor, do you think the injuries could have been self-inflicted?'

'No, I do not. Some of the injuries could be explained by an accident, but not all of them.'

'So, Professor, is it your opinion that the deceased women died because of throttling?'

'Yes.'

'And that gross violence had been used?'

'Yes. I believe so.'

'Might the scratches have been caused by a human hand?', the Advocate-Depute enquired.

'Yes, that is my view.'

'Might they have been caused by forcible contact with a blunt instrument?'

'Yes, that is also possible.'

'Very well. Please continue, Professor.'

'There was also a quantity of alcohol in the deceased woman's blood. However, I was unable to state with any degree of accuracy when that alcohol had been consumed. In addition, my post-mortem examination could not eliminate whether the grip of the victim's throat had been accidental. In my opinion there had been a constraint of the tissues of the neck, caused by the use of a right hand. However, it is not my province to say under what circumstances that may have occurred.'

Lord Carmont interjected at this point, clearly feeling that the jury required further clarity in the medical evidence:

'Professor, do I understand you to mean if somebody took the deceased by the neck, without meaning to kill her, the grip of the neck in itself might have accidently done so?'

'Yes, my Lord.' the Professor confirmed.

Sinclair Shaw now prepared the ground for the introduction of a macabre and dramatic piece of evidence into the trial:

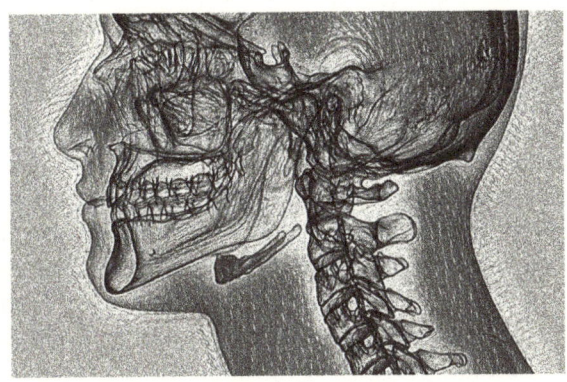

'May I introduce into evidence Exhibit B, the deceased woman's hyoid bone, which was removed during the post-mortem examination. Professor, please explain the significance of this evidence for the court.'

'Certainly. The hyoid bone is a U-shaped bone in the neck, which supports the tongue.'

'And what is unusual about the deceased woman's hyoid bone, Professor?'

'As you can, the bone has a degree of undue mobility – which is not normally present – and which could only be produced by pressure and counter pressure.'

'And what would be the result of such damage to a person's hyoid bone?'

'That person may develop rapid hemoptysis (a coughing up of blood from the lungs), edema (swelling caused by too much blood trapped in the tissues), and spasm, resulting in life threatening asphyxia, if not treated immediately.'

'Thank you, Professor. No further questions.'

It was now time for the defence to cross-examine Professor Glaister. The contest between Cameron and the medical expert proved to be something of a battle, as the two men clashed over the Professor's assessment regarding the actual cause of death. Eventually Lord Carmont was forced to adjourn proceedings until the following morning. Archibald Wood was returned to Perth Prison and Perth High Court was emptied.

Once again queues formed along Tay Street as the trial recommenced on the morning of Wednesday, 17 December 1947. Now on the back foot, after the dramatic introduction of the victim's hyoid bone into the trial, John Cameron KC continued his unfinished cross-examination by attacking Professor Glaister's conclusions regarding the cause of death:

'Surely, Professor, if the deceased lady had fallen in such a way, perhaps during a dizzy spell, would this not have produced a similar result to the hyoid bone?'

'I disagree,' retaliated Professor Glaister, 'If she had fallen violently on a V-shaped rough surfaced object, as you suggest, the injuries found on the neck would have been more definite and much more ragged in appearance, than those we did find.'

'And yet, Professor, Dr Myles pointed out that the usual

signs of asphyxia are not present in this case?'

'If I had had any doubt as to the cause of death, I would certainly have insisted on making further investigations, but I really did not feel there was anything more.'

'Tell me, Professor, did you not for example, think about the metal springs in the mattress and the degree of pressure and counter pressure which they might have produced on the neck of the victim during a fall?'

'No, I did not.'

'That does appear somewhat lax, in my opinion.' retorted the defence advocate, before quickly changed tack, in an effort to wrongfoot the witness, 'Tell me, Professor, you have heard Dr Myles' testimony in which he stated that Mrs Wood suffered from anaemia and that she had been ill-nourished.'

'Yes.'

'Surely then, Professor, these factors along with the fact that she was in the early stages of pregnancy, might make her subject to dizzy turns?'

'It is a possibility.' answered Professor Glaister.

'You have told this court, Professor, that in your opinion death occurred as a result of asphyxia?'

'Yes. In my medical opinion, death resulted from the effects of compression of the tissues of the neck.'

'Then, Professor Glaister, how do you then account for Dr Myles' observations in his report, and I quote, "that there was no protuberance of the eyes, no protrusion of the tongue, and no injuries to the mouth of the victim." Isn't it true to say that these are all common signs one might usually expect to see in cases of strangulation?'

'It is unusual, however, the absence of certain obvious signs of strangulation on the body could be accounted for by the fact that the heart had ceased to function before these could develop.'

'Very well, Professor, but I also put to you the suggestion that this woman's injuries might have just have easily been caused by a fall against a bed or a chair?'

With John Cameron's cross-examination having reached an impasse, Lord Carmont indicated to the opposing advocates that it was now time for the defence to cease their cross-examination and present their own case. John Cameron reluctantly acquiesced. He then revealed to the court that the defence would only be calling two witnesses to testify – the accused man's parents. Archibald Wood himself would not be called.

First to give evidence was Mrs Annie Wood, who gave her address as 20 Newmonthill, Forfar, and explained that 'Archie is my second of my three boys. Archie's health throughout his life has not been very good. He was poorly at school, and during his service in the Army he was discharged on medical grounds. After that he obtained work on the railway at Justinhaugh.'

'And tell the court about your son's habits, Mrs Wood.' Cameron asked.

'He was a heavy sleeper and, when he lived at home, I always had great difficulty in rousing him in the morning. I frequently called out to him two or three times, but he always fell asleep again.'

'So, it is possible, then, Mrs Wood, that he may not have heard his wife fall during the night of her death?'

'It is, Sir. He could sleep through anything.'

'Very well. Moving on then. Can you recall your daughter-in-law ever having any dizzy turns in your presence?'

'Yes,' Mrs Wood replied, 'She dropped down at the fireside one night. That was when she was pregnant with their first child. She just fell without any warning. Then, about six weeks later, when we were having tea, she suddenly fainted at the table.'

'Thank you, Mrs Wood. And did your son's wife ever speak to you regarding any difficulties in their marriage?'

'No. She never complained about Archie's behaviour to me.'

The Advocate-Depute, Mr Sinclair Shaw, cross-examined the witness at this point, 'Mrs Wood, were you on good terms with your daughter-in-law?'

'Yes, we were on friendly terms.'

'And how often did you see your daughter-in-law?'

'I did not see her very much.'

'Ah, that is what I thought. Thank you. No further questions.'

The final witness to be sworn in was the accused man's father, also named Archibald Wood. He confirmed the two occasions (already referred to by his wife) on which his daughter-in-law had fainted. He also added:

'She never complained about being bashed or knocked about. On the day when she died, our son came home to tell us. He was crying like a child and was very distressed. He loved Isabella.'

Unusually, after giving their respective statements, Archibald Wood's parents left the courtroom immediately and returned home to Forfar. They did not remain to hear the outcome of the trial.

Following this testimony, Mr Cameron KC concluded the case for the defence, hoping that he had demonstrated enough doubt in his client's guilt to allay a murder conviction. It was now time for the summations before releasing the jury to consider their verdict.

Following closing addresses from the two opposing advocates, Lord Carmont instructed the jury:

'Members of the jury, the defendant has pled "Not guilty" to the charge of murdering the deceased woman, and to previously repeatedly beating, assaulting and threatening to strangle her. There are four elements, or chapters, in this case which merit your deliberation. The first chapter to take into consideration was the state of relations between the deceased woman and the defendant, including the various statements which you have heard regarding the threats and actions by the accused man directed against his wife. The second chapter is a small one regarding Friday, September 12th. Witnesses have spoken of seeing the deceased woman alive for the last time, and also of seeing the accused. You must consider the importance of these in relation to what we now know happened next.

The third chapter relates to the events upon the following morning, when the accused man came out of his house and said that he had found his wife dead.

The final chapter to reflect upon is the expert evidence of the medical witnesses, supporting the case laid out by the Crown. These chapters are all of importance, and I think there is a peculiar importance to be attached to the chapter of evidence which deals with the relations of the accused and his wife. As you can well imagine, the light that can be cast upon subsequent events by the past history of their relations should be considered to be very important. This evidence,' continued Lord Carmont, 'has shown that the accused man possessed a bad temper. You must decide whether he said things he did not mean and did not, in reality, intend to act upon, or did his disposition instead show violence and, therefore, did he really mean something by the threats he made?

Crucially, and finally, I refer you to the morning of the tragedy, when the accused told the police that he had wakened at six o'clock, but he was not seen by his neighbour for another fifty-five minutes. What occurred during that missing fifty-five minutes? An explanation of what was happening in the cottage during that time may have been useful. Alas, we do not have one. There is only one person alive who can tell us what really took place within the walls of that house between the door closing at ten o'clock the previous night and five-to-seven the following morning. Therefore, you must ask yourselves the following – How did Archibald Wood spend his time between the discovery of his wife's death and when he stepped out of the cottage at 6.55am? Why did he take so long before he emerged? And does this bear on the case? In a case such as this, where no witness has seen what has occurred, one is entirely dependent on circumstantial evidence – evidence of facts and the inferences drawn from these facts.'

Before dismissing the jury, Lord Carmont issued a final

piece of advice regarding any potential verdict, 'Professor Glaister's post-mortem report has ruled out suicide or accident as a cause of death. Therefore, you must consider whether this poor woman's death was brought about by foul means and, if you believe that is the case, whether the Crown has proven, beyond reasonable doubt, that the defendant committed this crime. On the other hand, if you believe the case has not been proven you must find the defendant not guilty or, at the very least, his guilt not proven. The defence has argued that the injuries may have been inflicted accidentally, perhaps by a fall, or by the sharp springs of an old mattress. Is this explanation a plausible possibility for the cause of death, and, if so, does it cast reasonable doubt on this man's guilt? On the other hand, if you believe this woman died as the result of an attack, was that assault reckless, was it murder, or did it fall short of the definition of that most heinous of crimes? Members of the jury, will you please retire and consider your verdict.'

Throughout the three-day trial, Archibald Wood had sat passively in the dock. However, as he was led away to await the fruits of the jury's deliberations, a flicker of emotion could be detected on his face.

After an absence of 30 minutes a communication was sent from the jury room to Lord Carmont. Further clarification regarding the legal definition, under Scottish law, of murder and of culpable homicide, was requested. The information was duly provided:

'Murder occurs when a person takes the life of another either deliberately, with intent, or in circumstances where the accused person exhibits reckless disregard for the life of their victim. Culpable Homicide is the *Actus Reus* (wilful act) of killing a person in circumstances which are neither accidental nor justified, but where the wicked intent to kill or wicked recklessness required for murder is absent.'

Another 30 minutes passed, as the crowd in the public gallery and on Tay Street outside waited in eager anticipation.

Finally, a signal was sent that the jury had reached a verdict and the prisoner was sent for.

'Members of the jury, have you reached a verdict in this case?'

'We have, your Honour.'

'And how do you find the defendant?'

'Guilty of culpable homicide.'

Archibald Wood fell backwards and was steadied by two guards as his advocate, John Cameron KC requested the opportunity to address Lord Carmont in his chambers prior to sentencing. Cameron spoke eloquently on his client's behalf:

'Your Honour, this is Mr Wood's first time before a court. His intellectual development is not high and his health poor. Yet he volunteered to do his bit, and served in the army until March 1942, when he was discharged due to ill-health. He was then married in December of that year. There were three very young children from their union. Though Mr Wood was a cheerful, happy and obliging worker, his home life did not appear to have been very happy. There were clearly faults on both sides in their marriage.

The medical evidence in this case has been challenged and it is clear that my client was unfortunate in striking a vital spot, sadly bringing about the death of his wife. We earnestly request that you consider all these factors, and are duly lenient in your sentencing of Mr Wood. Thank you, your Honour.'

Archibald Wood was ordered to stand as the judge re-entered the courtroom. Although Wood had avoided the death penalty (it would not be removed from the statute book, for this type of offence, until the passing of the Murder Act 1957), the possibility of a severe sentence – even life imprisonment – still loomed over the convicted man.

Lord Carmont addressed Wood:

'Prisoner at the bar; there is no doubt that the jury has taken a lenient view of the evidence presented in this case. In the sentence I have given full effect to the nature of the crime and to everything that has been said on your behalf. The sentence of this court is one of penal servitude (hard labour) for ten years. Take him away.'

Archibald Wood was taken away to begin his incarceration in Perth Prison. He served the majority of his ten-year sentence, before being released on licence in 1954. Wood returned, not to Justinhaugh, but to his parents' home in Newmonthill, Forfar, where he managed to obtain employment with the textile firm, Moffat & Co, in South Street. He eventually passed away in 1984 at the age of 64, by which time he was living in the Kilmarnock area.

There is one more interesting twist in the story of Archibald Wood, especially for those who believe in poetic justice or even in divine retribution. While employed at Moffat & Co, he suffered a serious work-related injury during June of 1955. Wood's right arm became trapped in large commercial mangle, resulting in his right hand being severely damaged. Despite the efforts of surgeons at Dundee Infirmary, Wood never regained the use of his right hand – the same one which he had used to assault and strangle his wife almost a decade earlier.

13 – THE CRIEFF TRIANGLE

January 1981 – Muthill farmer Alexander McNicol had recently discovered that his wife, Judy, was involved with another man. As is often the case in these matters, many others were already fully aware of the affair. Now, weighed down with the financial worries of a failing farm, two young children, and the prospect of impending public humiliation, McNicol felt he had only two choices. Make one last attempt to save his ailing marriage, or take his own life.

On Saturday, 10 January 1981 he sat down alone to watch television at Mill of Drummond Farm, the family's home near Muthill in Perthshire. It was a cold January night. The McNicol's two children were in bed and Judy had gone out for the evening. Alexander did not know where, but he suspected her explanation that she was 'just going out with friends' was not true.

He flicked between the three channels, searching for a suitable programme to watch. At last, he settled on a TV movie about a couple who had committed suicide, after a series of personal catastrophes. Hardly a cheerful film, but it perfectly matched his mood. At that moment McNicol decided to take his own life. He took a large calibre .44 revolver – the same handgun which had been glamourised in the recent series of *Dirty Harry* movies featuring Clint Eastwood – from his gun cupboard and loaded it. McNicoll maintained a keen interest in shooting and had several licensed weapons. In 1981, six years prior to the Hungerford massacre in England, the registration of firearms was far more relaxed than it is today.

After picking up the revolver, fully intending to shoot himself, he had a sudden change of heart when he contemplated the effect of his actions on his family. He carefully placed the revolver inside a cupboard in the adjoining room. Crucially, however, he left the weapon fully loaded.

The story of the tragedy that was about to unfold really begins a decade earlier. Judith Bannister had moved to the Crieff area from Leeds in the early 1970s, after the death of her first husband in a car crash. Before long she obtained a job as a receptionist at the Lochearnhead Hotel. Then aged 21, she soon met Alexander McNicol and the couple married in 1973. Within four years a son and daughter were born. Now with young children to bring up, the unsociable hours at the hotel no longer suited Judith and she took employment at the Crieff branch of the Huddersfield and Bradford Building Society opposite the Town Hall and Clocktower. There she met the manager, 29-year-old Ronald Beveridge.

Mr Beveridge was three years younger than Judith and, in addition to being popular among the staff, was a keen sportsman and local Rotarian. Although married, he was now separated from his wife. Soon after Judith's appointment at the building society, an affair started between the couple. Rumours inevitably began to spread and, before long, Alexander McNicol discovered the truth. He contacted Ronald Beveridge and demanded that the two men meet to clear the air. Beveridge appears to have initially refused, however, after McNicol threatened to contact Beveridge's superiors at the building society and inform them of the affair, Beveridge reluctantly agreed to the meeting. McNicol insisted that Beveridge 'come to the farm so the three of us can sort this out,' and added, 'if you don't, I'll ask that you be transferred to another branch so your affair with my wife will be ended.'

On the morning of Monday, 12 January 1981, after the McNicol's children had left for school, Ronald Beveridge arrived at the Mill of Drummond Farm. It seems that McNicol may have changed his mind about the awkward meeting, as he initially refused to allow Beveridge inside, but eventually agreed. McNicol, his wife, and her lover than sat down to discuss the fallout from the affair. Only one person would emerge alive from that room, leaving us with just a solitary version of events. That version would later emerge at the High Court in Perth.

What we do know, with any degree of certainty, is that McNicol left the room as the exchanges between the three parties became heated. Once out of the room, he removed the still-loaded .44 Magnum handgun from the cupboard in the adjacent room (which had remained where he had placed it two days earlier). He then returned to the sitting room and emptied the chamber, firing six shots at point blank range, killing Judy and her lover instantaneously. McNicol then took another revolver (a .28 calibre pistol) from his gun cabinet and got into his car. Intent on suicide, he drove away from the farmhouse but quickly returned to lock the premises, as he realised that the two bodies would be discovered by his children when they returned from school.

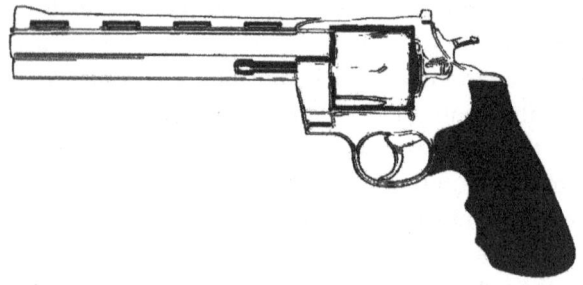

Still proposing to take his own life, McNicol then drove around for an hour or so, before telephoning the family's solicitor, David Graham. McNicol indicated that he intended to commit suicide and that he had 'done something serious.' Graham persuaded him to come immediately to his office and, on learning of the tragic events, instantly called for an ambulance (in case the two victims were still alive). Then, after persuading McNicol against suicide, he took him to the police station in Crieff, where McNicol confessed to killing his wife and her lover. He was subsequently arrested and charged with 'assaulting Judith McNicol, and Ronald Beveridge, of 6 Cairn Court, Crieff, in the farmhouse at Mill of Drummond on Monday 12th January, and that you did discharge a firearm at them and murder them.'

When a photograph of McNicol wearing sunglasses appeared in the tabloids, the comparison with Clint Eastwood's Dirty Harry added another layer of sensation to the tragic case.

After an initial court hearing in front of Sheriff John Wheatley, in which McNicol entered a plea of 'not guilty' to murder, it was intimated by his solicitor that he would be prepared to plead guilty to the lesser charge of culpable homicide in the case of each victim. A trial date was then set for Tuesday, 28 April 1981 at the High Court in Perth.

This would allow time for McNicol's mental state to be assessed as he remained on 'suicide watch' at Perth Prison. When the date for the trial finally arrived, the courthouse in Perth was buzzing with anticipation, the crowd all anxious to witness the 'Crieff Love Triangle Murderer', as McNicol had been labelled by one of the more salacious newspapers. The trial was also a chance to unveil the new Court No 3, which had been constructed on the upper storey of the building. However, the jostling press and public were to be disappointed, as it was ordered that they be first cleared from the courthouse to allow the prisoner to be escorted from Perth Prison, through the rear entrance to the building, and via a private enclosed stairway to take his position in the dock.

Lord Ian Robertson presided over the trial, while the Advocate-Depute, A C M Johnston QC, represented the Crown's interests. Alexander McNicol was represented by Herbert Kerrigan QC and his solicitor David Graham. The courtroom was hushed in expectation as the accused man entered a plea of 'not guilty' to the double murder of Judith McNicol and Ronald Beveridge, but 'guilty' to a reduced charge of culpable homicide on the grounds of diminished responsibility at the time of the crime. Lord Robertson indicated that legal arguments would now be heard before the court could decide if such a plea was to be accepted. Lord Robertson had notably presided in the 1974 trial of a Glasgow nurse, Jessie McTavish – 'The Angel of Death' – accused of murdering or assaulting five patients. Lord Robertson's failure to mention certain evidence during his summation in that case led to McTavish's sentence being overturned on appeal. In the case of Alexander McNicol, and with huge media attention levelled on the trial, there could be no repeat of this error.

Johnston then opened with the case for the prosecution, 'Ronald Beveridge was the manager of the Huddersfield and Bradford Building Society in Crieff, where Mrs McNicol a mother of two also worked. It is accepted by the Crown that the accused had been under various personal pressures, including financial problems, but more importantly the discovery that his wife had been having a sexual relationship with Mr Beveridge. Mr McNicol was also aware that other people had known of the affair. When Mr Beveridge left the building society office that morning, he told his staff that he would be away for about an hour on a matter of a personal nature.'

The prosecution then went on to describe the tragic events that occurred at the Mill of Drummond farmhouse on the morning in question:

'When Mr Beveridge reached the farmhouse, we understand that the trio engaged in a discussion which continued for about half an hour before it was terminated by the shootings. According to the statement made by the accused, during these discussions, Mr Beveridge taunted him with his inability to adequately satisfy his wife sexually. McNicol then struck him with a telephone before going to another room where he took a loaded .44 revolver from his gun cabinet. He must then have returned to the other room and immediately used the gun accurately, and also to some extent indiscriminately, based on the number of shots fired. From the position in which the victims were found it seems that neither appreciated what was about to happen. Mrs McNicol had three bullet wounds, Beveridge had been shot twice, and the bullet from the gun's sixth chamber was found embedded in a piece of kitchen equipment. There had clearly been provocation just before the event and psychiatrists had concluded that the accused had gone into some sort of uncontrollable frenzy.'

Johnston then paused to hold up the fearsome revolver, before continuing his address:

'This weapon is just about the heaviest type of revolver now available. It has a very considerable recoil and to that extent would not be accurate unless handled by a person of considerable skill. Because of the effect of recoil, it would have to be re-aimed after each shot. The accused must have re-aimed each time to achieve the results he did, and his psychiatrists have attached importance to the fact that in each case one or more shots struck the lower part of the victim's body. This may have been some sort of sexual revenge for the taunting.'

Johnston concluded the prosecution's case by stating:

'Although the Crown has accepted the plea to the lesser charges, we do not regard the shootings as justifiable killings or anything like that. The use of a firearm in such circumstances cannot he condoned and two people are dead as a result of the actions of this man. The Crown does not consider this to be anything other than an extremely serious crime.'

With the evidence for the prosecution now completed, Herbert Kerrigan QC stood up to address the court.

In a speech lasting almost an hour he emphasised that his client 'had personality difficulties as well as serious financial difficulties. The latter had stemmed from taking over the farm when it already had a £3,000 overdraft. Despite my client's best-efforts things had gone from bad to worse. Eventually the bank pressed him to reduce his considerable overdraft and he faced the very real threat of the farm having to close down within a very short period of time. It was against this background that the accused's marriage started to break down.

Initially the two couples had gone out as a foursome but Mrs Beveridge had discovered the affair last summer and left her husband. Mr McNicol had his suspicions but for a long time his wife denied that anything was going on. Eventually, however, he discovered that she had not been attending "keep-fit" classes, as she had told him, and a day or so before her death confessed to the affair for the first time.

Now, it is important to appreciate that Mr McNicol's marriage had been his haven of security and happiness, and it was the threat to this which had led to the tragedy. On 10th January he had watched a TV film about a couple who committed suicide. In a state of deep depression he then decided to take his own life. He loaded the .44 revolver with the intention of using it to kill himself. But because of the effect this would have had on his family he changed his mind. Only for this reason was the gun still loaded two days later when Mr Beveridge insisted on calling at the farm.

There is no indication whatever that the defendant plotted to kill the lovers. It is also clear that he had not lured Beveridge to the farm, but that it was Beveridge who had insisted on calling there to discuss the situation with the McNicols, because he (Beveridge) wanted to settle the matter once and for all.[2]

Mr Beveridge made the fatal visit, however, after McNicol telephoned him and threatened to contact his superior at the building society and advise him about the affair. When Mr Beveridge arrived McNicol initially tried to keep him out but eventually let him in. Mr Beveridge then began his cruel taunts alleging – quite wrongly – that McNicol was not sexually adequate to cope with his wife's needs. He also taunted McNicol about losing his wife and said that he "was taking her away". The accused man may have been over-possessive. Indeed, he may have been over-jealous, but his relationship with his wife was very precious to him and he realised it was ending. It was in light of these circumstances that he committed these acts. He has no recollection of the precise circumstances other than he went out of the room and obtained the weapon, which he had originally intended using upon himself. He then returned to the other room and used the weapon. Thereafter he took another revolver, a .28, and got into his car again, intent on suicide. He drove away from the farmhouse but then returned to secure the premises so that the bodies would not be found by the children when they returned from school. Still intending suicide, he contacted Mr Graham, his solicitor, bringing us to the circumstances in front of his Lordship today.'

In his final summation Kerrigan added that his client, 'would suffer for the rest of his life in the knowledge that he had taken the life of the one he loved. Mr McNicol had hoped to become a policeman, but followed his father as a farmer, when he failed to pass the police medical. Later in life he was able in some small way to satisfy his ambition by joining the Special Constabulary and devoting a number of years' service without any adverse reports.

I maintain that public interest does not require a prison sentence in such a tragic case and I suggest that the accused man should be put on probation so that he can rebuild his life and help bring up his now motherless children. Their future will not be enhanced by jailing their father.'

Following the summations Lord Robertson then delivered his verdict to the prisoner in the dock:

'Alexander McNicol, I note from the psychiatrists' report that there is no evidence of mental or psychiatric disorder, or unsoundness of mind. In the ordinary case, this would lead to a conclusion that there is insufficient evidence to justify this court concluding that diminished responsibility was a factor here.

The Crown, in this case, however, has already accepted that there was an extreme emotional crisis, coupled with provocation, of such magnitude as to justify acceptance of a culpable homicide plea. But it must be realised that you have pled guilty to killing two people and despite the background of mitigating circumstances this remains a most serious crime. Accordingly, the Court cannot take anything but a most serious view and there can be no question of a soft sentence. You will go to prison for nine years.'

Alexander McNicol staggered visibly as he was led away to begin his sentence and his solicitor, David Graham, announced to the awaiting press outside that his client would be launching an immediate appeal against his conviction.

McNicol was granted an appeal, which was heard a month later at the Court of Appeal in Edinburgh, by Lords Wheatley, Dunpark, and Grieve. Charles Kemp Davidson QC argued on McNicol's behalf that, at his original trial, Lord Robertson had allowed his personal view regarding the Crown's acceptance of a culpable homicide plea to influence the severity of his verdict, and that a greater reduction in sentence should have been granted bearing in mind both the reduced charges and the admission of guilt.

However, on this occasion the Court of Appeal would not overturn Lord Robertson's original verdict. Lord Wheatley gave judgement that the Appeal hearing felt that:

'It was quite clear from the trial judge's report that he had already implemented a reduction in sentencing on account of the reduced charges. McNicol could not have a reduction of sentence twice over. The factors sufficient in reducing the charges from murder were the same factors taken into account in deciding the appropriate sentence.'

The Appeal judges were also critical of Herbert Kerrigan's proposition to Lord Robertson, at the original trial, suggesting that probation might be a sufficient punishment. Lord Wheatley added:

'I can only regard that as a completely outlandish and unjustified proposal to a trial judge, suggesting that the interests of justice would have been served by disposing of this case by simply putting the accused on probation. This appeal is refused.'

Alexander McNicol was returned to prison to serve the remainder of his sentence.

Three years later, in an interesting aside to the story, a little-used Scottish legal precedent was utilised at the High Court in Perth. At the time of Judith McNicol's killing in 1981, Scottish law dictated that, when a wife or husband died without leaving a will, the surviving spouse was usually entitled to be appointed as executor to the dead partner's estate. However, following revelations that McNicol might somehow benefit from his wife's death, a special petition at Perth Sheriff's Court led to the rule being waived in the interests of the couple's children. Lord Wheatley, who had refused McNicol's appeal three years earlier, agreed with the petition and appointed a solicitor to oversee the estate instead.

In more recent years the legal loopholes allowing criminals to benefit from the dividends of their crimes have been largely closed through legislation such as the Proceeds of Crime Act 2002.

14 – THE WHITE TOWER MURDER
(Part One)

September 1947 – A little after 8am on the morning of Friday, 26 September 1947, one of the most violent murders in Scottish criminal history took place in a peaceful cottage tucked on a hillside in rural Perthshire.

With the war having finished two years earlier, life in the communities of Aberfeldy and Kenmore was slowly returning to normal. Although the majority hoped to put the worst memories of the war behind them, the residual effects of the conflict were there for everyone to see. Rationing continued, fuel was in short supply, and in Kenmore Polish soldiers were still stationed at Taymouth Castle, which was still requestioned by the War Office.

On the expansive Bolfracks Estate, among the trees on the southern hills overlooking Taymouth Castle, stood the distinctive White Tower. The McIntyre family lived in a cottage (known locally as Tower Cottage or The Towers) attached to the impressive gothic structure.

Peter McIntyre had been head-shepherd on the estate

since 1935, and had set off early that morning, bound for the Perth Sheep Sales in the Fair City. He had recently received his three-monthly pay packet, containing £80 in banknotes (approximately £4,000 today), which he had left with his wife, Catherine, for housekeeping. Aged 47, Catherine also helped on the estate, cleaning and cooking at the big house. Their son Archie, aged 22, was employed on a nearby estate and was hoping to join the police. Mary, their sixteen-year-old daughter worked as a typist in the Commercial Bank's Aberfeldy branch. She had already departed for work.

Left alone in the cottage, Catherine McIntyre (known to her friends and family as Cathie) was shortly due to go and light the fires at Tombuie, the house belonging to J Douglas Hutchinson, the owner of the Bolfracks Estate. He was expected to arrive at the estate later that day for a weekend of stalking, after having attended the Perth Hunt. Cathie stacked the breakfast dishes, ready to wash, and sat down to write two letters to her grown up daughters. Cathie looked up at the clock, knowing that if she finished the letters by 10 o'clock, she could hand them to the local postman John Shearer, who usually called at that time.

As Cathie sat down at the kitchen table, engrossed in her letters, she was completely unaware of a sudden movement outside in the tall bracken that bordered the track running down the hill from the cottage. A short, unkempt man had been hiding in the undergrowth there for several hours, intently watching the cottage while nervously gripping a shotgun in his hand. He had been patiently waiting for Peter McIntyre, Archie and Mary to leave for work. Mary had been last to leave, at 8.35am. Once the man was certain the family would not return, he moved cautiously towards the cottage. The McIntyres kept five dogs. Four were working dogs but were safely housed in their kennels. The fifth, a docile cairn terrier was in the cottage with Cathie. Perhaps the dogs barked on seeing the ragged stranger, or conceivably Cathie opened the door on hearing a noise. Perhaps the stranger even knocked the door, or forced his way in? We will never know. In any case, it is unlikely the door was locked.

The postman called later than usual, around 11.30am, and discovered the cottage locked. He left the newspaper and post on the step outside and left.

The next thing we know for certain is that at 4.30pm, John Keay, the coal merchant from Home Street in Aberfeldy arrived to make his regular delivery. The family's pet dog ran past him as he drove up the track. He found the cottage door locked. After knocking and receiving no answer, he too left.

Archie McIntyre returned home at 5.15pm, he was surprised to find both the back and front doors locked, the family's cairn terrier sat outside, and his mother apparently not at home. Archie then remembered that his mother was due to set the fires at Tombuie and was probably still there. He sat down on the step to read the newspaper.

However, shortly afterwards – around 5.30pm – the estate gamekeeper Clement MacKercher arrived at the cottage and told Archie that he could see no smoke coming from the chimneys at Tombuie. He enquired, 'Why has Cathie no been up to light the fires?'

'I don't know,' Archie responded.

Clement MacKercher informed Archie that his mother had also been expected to call on his wife for a cup of tea, and had not done so.

'I lent her my watch last evening,' the gamekeeper explained, 'as her watch was n' working, so there was no reason for her to be late today. I'm afraid she must have had an accident.'

'A very strange accident,' Archie replied, 'when both doors are locked.'

At this point Archie began to worry. With no key, and unable to get into the cottage, he decided to climb in through the kitchen window, using a small ladder which had been leaning against the wall. One inside the kitchen, he looked around. There, on the wooden table lay Cathie's glasses and the unfinished letters she had begun to write earlier that morning. No housework had been done and the breakfast dishes were still unwashed in the scullery. There was no sign of his mother. He searched the house and was surprised to find his own bedroom door locked (the internal doors in the cottage were never usually locked). Unable to find any keys, he picked up the wood axe, which had propped up by the front door, and forced the bedroom door open. As he did so, Archie was met by a gruesome and shocking sight. His mother lay on the bed, her body covered with a mattress, which had been dragged across from the other bed in the room. A scarf covered her face, and aprons had been tied around her neck. Her hands had been secured across her stomach with black bootlaces and her head savagely bludgeoned. Cathie's face was swollen and discoloured. Archie immediately sent MacKercher to call for the police while he searched in vain for the keys. Presumably, in an attempt to delay the discovery of the body, the assailant had locked the doors and taken the keys with him.

Due to the horrific nature of the crime, three of Scotland's most experienced and respected police officers attended the scene, Detectives William Ewing and Superintendent Gilbert McIlwrick from Glasgow, and Chief Constable A C Sim from Perth. Search teams from the Perth County Police were also drafted in. Under the supervision of Superintendent McIlwrick, officers were forced to break the glass panel in the front door and climb into the cottage. It was soon discovered that £80 (in white £5 notes), rationing coupons, Cathie's wedding ring, and a grey/blue man's suit had been stolen from the cottage.

Dr Charles Swanson, from Aberfeldy, was then called to examine the body. He estimated the time of death between 9am and 10am that morning.

Meanwhile the police began a widespread search of the surrounding countryside. It was initially suspected that a passing tramp or vagrant might be to blame. However, this line of enquiry was quickly dropped, when Archie McIntyre revealed that he had the impression someone, or something, may have been moving in the nearby bracken, as he had walked down the track to work earlier that morning. Unfortunately, he had dismissed it, as he was late for work, and assumed it to be a deer or other animal. The police immediately searched the undergrowth in the area McIntyre had described. They found an area of flattened foliage, indicated that someone had been lying there for a considerable time.

A further search of the hillside approximately 400 yards from the cottage revealed an area of tumbled stones, in which officers made several dramatic discoveries. The Chief Constable issued the following description of the items to the press – a manhunt was now in progress:

'Early this afternoon police officers engaged in the search on the hillside about 400 yards from Tower Cottage found, concealed among the bracken, the following articles which, in all likelihood, had been discarded and concealed by the murderer. A sawn-off twelve bore double-barrelled hammer shotgun -top lever opening – having the name Chas. Pryse on both sides; the figure "12" displayed inside a diamond, and the figure 13/T. The serial number on the gun is 64417-2. It appears to be an old gun and to have been shortened recently. Among other articles found was a twelve-bore cartridge, make Eley-Kynoch, and the following articles of clothing: A gentleman's gaberdine raincoat, raglan style, bluish grey in colour, roll and step collar, ribbed artificial silk dark grey coloured lining, to fit a man around five-foot nine inches to 5-foot ten inches in height. The sleeves had been lengthened about an inch when new. There are vertical pockets at the side, and the second and fourth buttons are missing. The top button is fastened with copper wire. The right pocket is torn at the bottom, the left pocket is also torn, but the tear has been sewn up. There is a small hole inside the right front of the coat, which has been sewn with canvas linen. There are three buttons on each sleeve. The coat is well worn, the collar is dirty and greasy and the cuffs frayed. In addition, my constables found a pair of blue bib and brace overalls. These are also well worn and dirty, with small tears in the front and inside of the left leg and on the rule pocket. They are frayed at the bottom.

A man dressed in dirty working clothes, which appeared to correspond with the garments found on the hillside, was seen in the locality on Wednesday afternoon, two days before the murder. The police are anxious to obtain any information regarding this man as it is possible that he may have endeavoured to seek work at some of the farms or elsewhere in the district. Any person who may have seen the man is requested to communicate with the nearest police station. The police also want to know whether the shotgun found on the hillside has been stolen from some farm or outhouse and any information regarding it is urgently desired.'

A further description was also issued of a man's suit stolen from the cottage by the murderer:

'Gent's new blue-grey worsted suit (background predominantly blue) with white or light grey pin stripe. The stripes are exactly one inch apart. It is a single-breasted suit, with the usual pockets. The trousers have two side and hip pockets and the belt has a waist fastening with buttons.'

The police also discovered several other key items, that would help connect their owner to the murder. A bloodstained handkerchief, a safety razor (with hair still adhered to the blade) and (what would prove to be) a key piece of evidence – the return section of a railway ticket, issued the previous day, for a journey from Perth to Aberfeldy. Crucially, the ticket was of a special type, only issued to soldiers in uniform.

The revelation regarding the railway ticket helped the police narrow the search significantly. Interest now fell on Taymouth Castle, lying in the valley just below the cottage. Upwards of 800 Polish soldiers were still billeted there.

Nevertheless, exhaustive enquires at the castle failed to

produce any results. All soldiers were accounted for and none of the missing items were found. However, several witnesses remembered seeing a dishevelled man, whom they presumed to be a Polish soldier, in the vicinity earlier that day.

John Moir, owner of the General Merchants Shop in nearby Kenmore Square, described witnessing 'a scruffy looking man at around 11.45am. The man, who clearly could not speak much English, was enquiring about the times of buses to Aberfeldy.'

Wilhelm Horn (a German prisoner-of-war, working nearby) also spotted the same shabby figure, anxiously clutching a satchel, waiting for the bus.

Janet Pringle from Acharn, a conductress on the bus from Killin to Aberfeldy, witnessed the same man board the noon Aberfeldy-bound bus from Kenmore. Witnesses in Aberfeldy were then able to describe what appeared to be an identically dressed man hailing a taxi from Aberfeldy to Perth shortly after getting off the bus. The taxi driver recalled that the man paid the fare from a large roll of banknotes. From the various witness statements, a detailed description of the suspect was issued without delay:

'About 35 years of age, slim build, thin face, pointed chin and clean shaven, suffers from a spasmodic cough.'

With the realisation that the wanted man, now with money in his pocket and having reached Perth, could have conceivably travelled by train or bus anywhere in the country, detectives could only hope that someone would recognise him – before he escaped abroad, or even worse, killed again.

Fortunately for the authorities, they would not have long to wait. The lucky break would come just 48 hours later, and over 100 miles away. Mrs Isabella Clubb, from Tulloch Farm in Aberdeenshire, immediately recognised the description of the shotgun and of the man. She telephoned Aberdeen Police with the details of a Polish ex-soldier called Stanislaw Myszka, who had worked on the farm from June until mid-September. On 18 September, according to Mrs Clubb, Myszka had informed her that he was leaving with the intention of travelling to Perthshire to search for work. Shortly after he had left their employment, the family noticed that a shotgun from the farm was missing.

The Perth Police also received a telephone call from a Scottish girl, married to a Polish soldier from Taymouth Castle. She remembered seeing Myszka suddenly appearing in Aberfeldy, with a role of white £5 notes.

Now, with a name to match their description, detectives intensified their manhunt. During the morning of 2 October police constables were searching a cluster of disused RAF buildings, at Longside near Peterhead. One of the men, Constable McLaren, saw a man running from one of the huts across the fields. The officers immediately gave chase. After three quarters of a mile they apprehended the man, who was attempting to hide under a bush. In his possession were six £5 banknotes, three £1 notes, ten shillings and nine pence in coins, together with a number of rationing coupons. When asked his name the man simply replied 'Myszka.' He was arrested and then searched at the Peterhead Police Station. Hidden in the insole of his left shoe was Cathie McIntyre's wedding ring.

Myszka, who had deserted from the Polish Resettlement Corp, did not have the physical appearance of the monster that the public and the arresting officers were anticipating. He was a small, insignificant and unassuming man, dressed in an ill-fitting suit, only 5 feet 2 inches in height.

Stanislaw Myszka was taken to Perth, and placed before Sheriff Prain to be formally charged. The courthouse on Tay Street was heavily guarded and police officers lined the street as a large crowd jostled, all anxious for their first glimpse of the brutal murderer who had been on the loose for seven days. Via a Polish interpreter Myszka, who spoke only a little English, was charged with the murder of Catherine McIntyre. A trial date was set for Tuesday, 6 January at the High Court in Perth.

As seems to be the case with all major murder trials, there

was a great deal of public interest in the case. From daybreak, long queues formed outside the courthouse, with huge numbers anxious to witness the proceedings. When asked to answer the charge by Lord Sorn, Myszka, wearing a smart grey suit with a collar and tie, pled 'not guilty' to murder (with a 'special defence' which would be introduced by his advocate), but 'guilty' to the lesser charge of stealing a shotgun. A secondary theft charge was also added, to include the other items stolen from Tower Cottage – a pair of earrings, two rings, a watch, five clothing coupon books and £85 in cash. Myszka also pled 'guilty' to these offences. A Polish Army officer was provided to translate for the accused man.

The prosecution, led by Harold R Leslie KC, the Advocate-Depute for Perthshire, indicated that the Crown would be producing in court 'A total of seventy-five pieces of evidence and forty-two witnesses.' However, before he was permitted to begin the case for the prosecution, Stanislaw Myszka's advocate, F C Watt KC, dramatically introduced a special plea on behalf of the defendant.

15 – THE WHITE TOWER MURDER (Part Two)

'Your honour,' Mr Watt began, 'it had been originally intended at the pleading diet to enter a plea that Mr Myszka was insane and not capable of instructing his defence. That has now been withdrawn. Following medical advice, my client is now pleading not guilty with a special defence that he was insane at the time of the alleged crimes and therefore not responsible for his actions.'

Mr Leslie, for the Crown, offered no objection to this change in plea, although he did call Dr Jan Leyberg, the senior Polish medical officer from the Argyll and District Mental Hospital to the stand.

'Dr Leyberg, you examined Stanislaw Myszka. I understand you are an expert in cases of insanity?'

'Yes,' replied the doctor, 'I have specialised in psychiatry for ten years.'

'Thank you, Dr Leyberg. And your conclusions after examining the prisoner?'

'I examined him on October 7th last year and talked to him in his own language. I discovered no sign of mental disease or aberration at all. He was co-operative and coherent throughout and almost certainly sane then, and had been sane on September 26th. If he had done something wrong on September 26th, he would, in my opinion, have known exactly what he was doing, and that what he was doing was wrong.'

Dr Leyberg's findings were also confirmed by Dr Charles Bruce, the medical superintendent at the Criminal Lunatic Asylum in Murthly.

Their evidence alone, seemed enough to stifle the defence's special plea of insanity. Nevertheless, Mr Watt would have the opportunity to present Stanislaw Myszka's case later. In the meantime, it was time for the prosecution to continue.

The next witness to be called to the stand was Archie

McIntyre, the victim's son, who had recently joined the City of Edinburgh Police, his decision to do so no doubt accelerated by his mother's tragic murder.

'I left for work about eight o'clock in the morning, just behind my father.' he testified, 'My sister Mary and my mother were the only people left in the cottage. When I left, my mother was in the kitchen. She was very well at that time. I had lunch at work and I did not return to the cottage until approximately a quarter past five.'

'What first struck you when you reached the cottage, Mr McIntyre?'

'Our little cairn terrier was outside barking, Sir. I thought she was just barking at me because she was in the habit of barking at anyone who came out to the house. Then I noticed the newspapers on the doorstep, which were delivered by the postman and I thought it rather strange that the postie should leave the papers there.'

'Why did you think that strange?'

'Well, I knew my mother was going to go to Tombuie, but not till the afternoon of that day, so I thought she should have been there to take the papers in when they were delivered.'

At this point in the proceedings, the defence advocate subtly attempted to earn his client a degree of sympathy with the jury, by objecting to Lord Sorn that the court-appointed Polish interpreter was failing in his duty:

'Your honour, I have so far not heard the interpreter say a single word to the accused man!'

Would the defence's attempt to create the impression of a lonely and isolated figure in the courtroom, someone unable to comprehend the proceedings, be enough to win the jury's sympathy? It was a clearly a predetermined tactic on the part of the defence. Only time would tell if it would be a successful one.

Lord Sorn glanced sternly at the interpreter, before answering:

'Mr Watt, none of the evidence given so far is likely to

require an answer by the accused. However, I will maintain a close eye on points which ought to be made known to your client.'

The judge then instructed the interpreter – in no uncertain terms – to ensure that all the evidence and testimony was translated fully for Mr Myszka. With that minor interruption the trial was then allowed to continue.

After Archie McIntyre had described the details of his gruesome discovery on that tragic day, to which the jury of eleven men and four women appeared both shocked and repulsed, he was shown the first exhibit of evidence – his missing pinstripe suit which had been found in the accused man's possession.

'Do you recognise this suit, Mr McIntyre?'

'Yes, it is my suit, which I noticed was missing from the cottage. There were a pair of earrings, which belonged to a friend of mine, in one of the pockets.'

'Are these the earrings?' asked Mr Leslie, producing the set of earrings also found Myszka's possession.

'Yes, they are, Sir.'

In cross-examination, Watt for the defence attempted to

create some doubt regarding the provenance of the suit found in the accused man's possession:

'Can you be certain, Mr McIntyre, that this is your suit? After all, there are no tailor's markings, nor any labels of any kind on it.'

'Well,' Archie McIntyre admitted, 'I know there is no label, but this suit has certain faults in the threading on one of the pockets, and mine had that.'

However, when Peter McIntyre, the victim's husband, and Clement MacKercher, the gamekeeper, both testified that the suit shown in evidence definitely belonged to Archie McIntyre the defence was forced to concede this point. They fared little better when the next witness, Mrs Clubb from Tulloch Farm in Aberdeenshire, recognised a bloodstained handkerchief, found close to the crime scene, as one she had given to Myszka while he was employed at the farm during the summer.

It was now time for the crucial medical evidence to be presented to the court.

Dr Swanson from Aberfeldy, who had first examined the body, was then called to take his place on the witness stand.

'Doctor, when did you arrive at Tower Cottage?'

'I arrived about 6.30pm, after receiving a telephone call from the police station in Aberfeldy.'

'And, from your initial examination, Doctor, were you able to estimate the time of death?'

'I concluded that the woman had died eight to nine hours previously. That would make the time of death sometime between nine and ten in the morning.'

Once again, the defence advocate endeavoured to create some doubt regarding the estimated time of death. If it could be established that Mrs McIntyre had died much later than 10am, say around noon, this would create some uncertainty in his client's guilt, as Myszka had been spotted in Kenmore around 11.30–11.45am.

He began his cross-examination by asking Dr Swanson, 'Doctor, would not the mattress, bed clothes and garments which had been placed over the victim, insulate the body some-what, making any estimation of the time of death inaccurate?'

'Yes, a mattress and bed clothes placed over a body would contribute to heat being retained in a body for a period of time.'

'So, is it consistent to say that the woman may have been killed much later than the estimate which you have given?'

'It is quite possible,' conceded Dr Swanson.

Although this admission by Dr Swanson provided the defence with a minor victory, five further witnesses on behalf of the Crown were presented, all of whom confirmed Myszka as the shabbily dressed man, with a roll of banknotes, that they had seen attempting to leave Aberfeldy on the day of Cathie McIntyre's murder. The discovery by police officers of several parts removed from the twelve-bore shotgun stolen from Aberdeenshire, together with a number of items found in the bracken lair close to Tower Cottage, also did little to help the accused man's case.

Next came the forensic evidence, so often crucial in murder trials. Two of Scotland's leading pathologists, Professor John Glaister from Glasgow University's Forensic Sciences Department, assisted by Dr Edgar Rentoul, who had worked jointly on the post-mortem at Perth Mortuary, presented a detailed report for the court:

'Our report,' Professor Glaister began, 'states that there were four lacerated wounds on the left side of the scalp, in the vicinity of the left ear, and the base of the skull was fractured. Death, in our opinion, was due to fracture of the base of the skull with subdural haemorrhage, the result of very considerable violence together with additional respiratory embarrassment.'

'Professor, please explain that term for the benefit of the jury.' Lord Sorn interjected.

'Yes, your honour. It is a state of rapid and shallow breathing, combined with diaphoresis – sweating – and palpita-tions. It is not to be confused with the word "embarrassment" in the traditional sense.'

'Thank you, Professor, please continue.'

'The injuries to the victim were perfectly consistent with having been made by an instrument such as the barrel section of a double-barrelled shotgun.'

'In addition,' Professor Glaister continued, 'I compared hairs taken from the safety razor found close to Tower Cottage with hairs shaved from Mr Myszka's face in Perth Prison. Their detailed and general structural characteristics were so similar as to suggest that they had come from a common source.'

In cross-examination, Watt KC, Myszka's defence counsel, seized on a gap in the forensic evidence:

'Besides hair, did you find the defendant's fingerprints on the razor blade?'

'I found no fingerprints on the razor.'

'And in the cottage?' Mr Watt enquired.

'No, there were no fingerprints belonging to the accused man in the cottage, although there were a large number of glove marks.'

'Glove marks? But surely, they might have been made by anyone wearing gloves, including the police officers?'

'Yes. That is possible.'

'So there would be no way, Professor, to conclude by whom, or indeed when, these glove marks had been made?'

'That is correct.'

'Thank you. No further questions.'

Mr Watt finished his cross-examination for the defence, sensing he had perhaps secured another minor victory in his attempt to undermine the prosecution's case against his client.

With that Leslie concluded the Crown's case by remarking to the jury that:

'These facts presented to you here, if you look at them together, can lead you to but one verdict on the charges of murder and theft. Guilty as charged.'

It was now time for Watt to present the case for the defence.

THE WHITE TOWER MURDER (Part Two)

He called only one witness, Dr Angus McNiven, the superintendent physician at Glasgow Royal Mental Hospital.

'Dr McNiven, when did you examine the defendant?'

'I examined Mr Myszka just a few days ago, on 1st January. When I did so, I directed my attention to two problems – whether the accused man was fit to plead, and whether he had been sane at the time of the alleged crime. I concluded that he was fit to plead.'

'Thank you, Dr McNiven. And would you say that he is of normal intelligence?'

'He is below normal intelligence,' the doctor replied, 'but not mentally deficient. I would say he was emotionally unstable.'

'When you have a combination of these two factors, Doctor, low intelligence and emotional instability, would you, or would you not, agree that it is more difficult for that person to control their actions?'

'I would agree,' answered Dr McNiven, 'Mr Myszka is a person who is liable to sudden impulses.'

Watt then summed up the case for the defence:

'My client had received upsetting news about his children in France, coupled with three days of sleeplessness and lack of food. Dr McNiven has demonstrated that the defendant is a man of low intelligence and emotional instability. In addition, the evidence in this case, far from pointing to my client, in fact points to a possible mistake of identity, and of the presumed time of death, and has resulted in a man being placed in the dock against whom a charge of murder should not lie. I think, members of the jury, you too are bound to come to that conclusion.'

Lord Sorn spent more than an hour in his summation of this difficult and complicated case:

'Members of the jury,' he began, 'could there be any other reasonable conclusion other than the murderer in this case hid in those bracken lairs, and that the shotgun was the weapon? The gun itself had been stolen from the farm where

137

the accused used to work. He had used it while working there.

Perhaps the most striking feature of this whole case was the earrings. Archie McIntyre had earrings in the pocket of his suit. The suit found in Aberdeenshire had a pair of earrings of the same kind in it. This must surely mean that the person who brought the suit to Aberdeenshire was the murderer. Next, I come to the question of who hid the watch belonging to Mr MacKercher, the gamekeeper, in the Aberdeenshire farmhouse? Who could have put it there except the man who took it from Tower Cottage?

Regarding the medical evidence, I have not been able to find anything in all of the medical evidence which lends any countenance to the idea that the accused man was insane on September 26th. Therefore, it is my duty to direct you to ignore the special defence plea of insanity in the case. The other defence of diminished responsibility, proposed by Mr Watt, I leave it to you, the jury. However, it is not enough for the defence to show that he is subnormal in certain respects, such as intelligence, emotional stability, and self-control. Members of the jury, if you are honestly satisfied the accused man belongs to that category of person bordering on insanity, you would be entitled to return a verdict of culpable homicide. Members of the jury, please now retire and consider your verdict.'

Stanislaw Myszka was returned to his cell to await their deliberations. His wait would not be a long one.

The Jury took less than twenty minutes to reach their verdict. Myszka was found guilty of murder as charged. Lord Sorn called the jury's decision 'a just and fair one.' He ordered the Polish interpreter to stand beside Myszka in the dock and translate the sentence to him. The judge then ordered that the sentence be carried out at Perth Prison on 6th February. The four-day trial was finally over.

Stanislaw Myszka took the news calmly and was taken away to await his execution. Unusually, in such a case, the defence advocate indicated that no appeal for clemency would be lodged. The sentence would be carried out.

Albert Pierrepoint, the famous hangman, journeyed from London to Perth Prison to undertake the grim task. It was to be the first execution in Perth since 1909 and the only execution of a foreigner on Scottish soil in the twentieth century. It would also prove to be the final execution to take place at Perth Prison. A group of just twelve people gathered outside the prison to await confirmation of Myszka's death. Following the execution a notice was pinned to the prison gate, signed by all those present and simply stating:

'Death, which was instantaneous, occurred at 8.02am. The body has been buried within the walls of the prison.'

It was also later confirmed by Canon John Coogan, a priest who had visited the condemned man shortly before his execution, that:

'He proceeded calmly to the scaffold, saying nothing, showing no emotion, and making no last-minute requests.'

The evidence against Stanislaw Myszka was certainly persuasive. In addition to the testimony of several eyewitnesses, the presence of the shotgun and the bloodstained handkerchief – both recognised by Mrs Milne – together, with the large amount of money found in the fugitive's possession, the earrings, the railway ticket and the clothing coupons all point strongly to his guilt. The crime was undoubtedly for financial gain and the presence of the shotgun and the wearing of gloves clearly showed cold-hearted premeditation and not insanity.

Stanislaw Myszka, aged only 23 at the time of the murder, had first arrived in Scotland in 1945, after spending several years in France, during which time he had married a Parisian lady. She gave birth to two daughters and the couple were, by all accounts, happy. However, during the early years of the German occupation he had been forced to work as a farm labourer and then in the notorious Nazi Labour Camps.

Following the liberation of France, Myszka joined the Polish Resettlement Corps and was stationed at Comrie in

Perthshire. It appears that he then deserted from Comrie one night and travelled to Aberdeenshire, where he became a farm labourer. Desperately short of money, and perhaps hoping to find sufficient funds to enable him to travel back to France to be reunited with his wife and children, he had undertaken the vicious attack on Cathie McIntyre.

Exactly how he knew about the presence of such a large amount of money in the lonely cottage remains a mystery. Local speculation at the time seemed to suggest that 'pub talk' may have been the reason. However, Myszka had only arrived in Kenmore from Perth a day earlier. Perhaps he had originally intended to break into the large estate house, Tombuie, instead? The real reason will never be known.

The crime had a long lasting and deep impact on the quiet Highland Perthshire community. Its notoriety lasting for many years. As late as 1965 a Polish farmworker named John Szewc (hoping to apply for British citizenship) used the fact that he had testified as a witness in Myszka's trial, to help influence his claim.

Catherine McIntyre was buried just a mile away from Tower Cottage, in the family's grave located in the picturesque graveyard surrounding Kenmore Church, overlooking Loch Tay. The scars created by the brutal murder would affect the local community for many years, ending the age-old Highland tradition of householders always leaving their doors unlocked.

16 – THE CASE OF THE BLOODY CUTLASS

March 1929 – The cutlass is a weapon usually thought of as an eighteenth-century naval sidearm or perhaps as a pirate's weapon of choice, favoured for its short, curved blade and sharpened cutting area. Robust enough to hack through heavy ropes, yet short enough for close quarters combat, the cutlass surprisingly resurfaced as the chilling murder weapon during a bitter twentieth-century domestic dispute in a Perth back street.

On Sunday, 24 March 1929, Police Constable John Pritchard was directing traffic at the junction of Perth High Street and South Methven Street. It had been a quiet evening, there were far fewer motor vehicles on the streets of Perth than there are today. Scotland's first traffic lights had only been installed in Edinburgh a year earlier, and they had yet to reach the Fair City. Suddenly, at 10.30pm, PC Pritchard was startled by the approach of a flustered elderly man. Sixty-five-year-old Charles Lamb rushed up to the constable and blurted out, 'Come quick, you're wanted at Canal Crescent.'

'What is it?' the officer asked.

'There's been a serious stabbing accident. I was showing Bannerman a cutlass, and he made to take hold of it, and it somehow entered his body.'

'A cutlass?' remarked PC Pritchard, taken aback.

'Yes.'

On arriving at 124 Canal Crescent, a stone cottage fronting onto the street, the constable found 45-old William Bannerman on the kitchen floor. He appeared to be severely injured. A large pool of blood engulfed his lower torso and legs, and a thin red trail ran from the kitchen into the bedroom. A frightened middle-aged woman was also present. PC Pritchard asked her, 'What caused this man's wound?'

The lady, Miss Williamina Young, the landlady, looked at

Charles Lamb. He then went into his bedroom and returned with a sheaved cutlass. As he pulled the weapon from its sheath fresh blood dripped from it. Despite the threatening appearance of the weapon, the police constable did not panic.

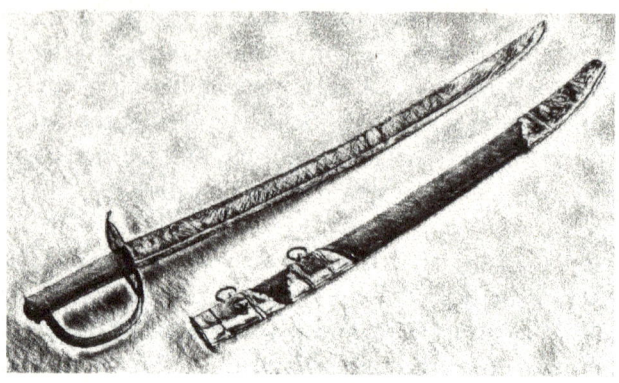

He ordered the inhabitants of the cottage to remain there, while he hurried away to fetch support and to summon a doctor. However, he was too late. On his return, William Bannerman was already dead. PC Pritchard promptly arrested Charles Lamb and escorted him to Perth Police Station.

Charles Lamb was brought before Sheriff-Substitute Robertson at the High Court and charged with William Bannerman's murder:

'In the house at 124 Canal Crescent, Perth, you did assault William Brough Bannerman, of 22 Thimble Row, Perth, did stab or cut him with a cutlass on the left groin, and did murder him.'

Charles Lamb responded with a plea of 'not guilty', claiming the whole event was a freak accident.

Lamb was a popular painter and decorator, well-known locally, and a member of the Perth branch of the Scottish Painters' Society. Dismayed at the arrest of one of their members, a campaign was quickly launched to raise money for Lamb's bail and to help with the cost of his defence. The following letter appeared in the *Perthshire Advertiser* the very next day:

'Dear Sirs

Please allow me space in your paper to make a strong appeal on behalf of Mr Charles Lamb, who is, as you are aware, in prison on a serious charge. I would ask you to voice our appeal as a trade union not as individuals with a view to other trades locally assisting. Mr Charles Lamb is a long standing and earnest member of our Society, hence our wish to assist him in his present position. I may say the above appeal is made with a view to raising a Defence Fund.

Donations to the above can be sent to President G. Maley. 132 High Street, Perth.'

Within a matter of days, a sum of £40 had been raised (approximately £3,200 today) and Charles Lamb was granted bail at a cost of £10. Thanks partly to pressure from his union and discussions with his advocate Robert Macgregor Mitchell KC, it was agreed to reduce the charge from one of murder to one of culpable homicide. Although this removed the threat of the death penalty for Lamb, culpable homicide was considered a very serious offence, and still carried the possibility of a life sentence.

A legal mistake in the wording on the indictment meant that Lamb's court appearance was delayed by several weeks. In the meantime, William Bannerman was buried at Wellshill Cemetery, Perth, in a private ceremony attended only by close family and friends.

Charles Lamb's delayed trial eventually opened at the High Court in Perth on Tuesday, 23 July 1929. Lord Moncrieff presided, while the much respected and usually formidable Thomas Murray Taylor prosecuted for the Crown. Taylor was a devout Christian who, no doubt, would have disapproved of the participants' behaviour in this 'love triangle' case. He would later become Principal of the University of Aberdeen, and Chair of the UK Commission for the Prevention of War. Charles Lamb was defended by Robert Macgregor Mitchell KC, a local man who had formerly served as the Liberal Member of Parliament for Perth.

Local feelings ran high on the day of the trial. Queues formed along Tay Street and South Street, everyone anxious to catch a glimpse of the protagonists in this strange affair. Perth's rumourmongers had been speculating for several weeks over the 'Sordid events in Canal Crescent' (as one newspaper claimed), and Perth Police were forced to sneak Charles Lamb into the courthouse via a side door on Canal Street, while crowds at the front were distracted by the arrival of an empty police wagon alongside the main entrance. Lord Moncrieff was ushered into court with the usual fanfare of trumpets, followed by the opening of proceedings with a prayer of dedication by the Reverend W G Lee from St John's Kirk.

Thomas Murray Taylor KC then began the case for the prosecution by describing the victim, William Bannerman, as a 'war hero who had served with The Black Watch during the Great War and was now employed as a lorry driver at Messrs Wordie & Company in Perth.'

He then questioned Miss Williamina Young in whose house the incident had taken place:

'Miss Young, please describe the arrangements at 124 Canal Crescent for the court.'

'Yes,' she began, 'The house consists of two rooms and kitchen. The room leading from the lobby was occupied by Mr Lamb. I knew the deceased man, William Bannerman, and I became acquainted with him about nine years ago. About two years ago he started visiting me at home. Usually at the end of each week. These visits were usually in the evenings, and we became very friendly. I knew he was a married man, but I did not know his wife.'

'Did you know that Mr Bannerman was in the habit of taking drink?'

'I did.'

'And knowing that, what did you do when you occasionally met him on the street?'

'I would ask him to come along to my house,' Miss Young replied.

'Was that with the view of taking him away from the temptation of drink?'

'It was.'

'Was there ever any drinking in your house when Bannerman was there?'

'Never.'

'Please explain to the court what happened on the night of Sunday 24th of March.'

'Along with my sister, I went to Saint Paul's Free Church. I am a member of the choir there. On the way home, I met Mr Bannerman in South Methven Street. He was alone and quite sober. We passed Charles Lamb in South Street on our way back, but he did not speak to us. Mr Bannerman came into the house, and we chatted but he was not drinking. About ten o'clock Mr Lamb entered the house and went into his room. He went straight back out again and slammed the door. I prepared a late supper, and while Mr Bannermen and I were eating Mr Lamb came back in. He indicated, in no uncertain terms, that Mr Bannerman should leave. Mr Lamb did not like him and did not approve of me meeting with a married man. I then suggested to Mr Bannerman that perhaps it was time that he left, after all. I accompanied him to the door and stood on the pavement talking to him for a while. While I was standing there, I noticed Mr Lamb's head sticking out of his bedroom window.'

'Did you say anything to me, Miss Young?'

'Yes, I said "What is the meaning of this?" to him.'

'And what happened then, Miss Young?' asked Taylor.

'Mr Bannerman said that he probably should go and bade me goodnight. I did wonder at that point whether Mr Lamb would say anything once I went back inside.'

'And what was Mr Lamb's reaction when he saw Mr Bannerman leaving?'

'He yelled, "Yes, go to your bed, you dirty devil!" Or some word like that.'

There was a murmur of amusement in the public gallery,

which caused the Advocate-Depute to pause his questioning of the witness momentarily.

'And did Mr Bannerman hear this remark?'

'He did, He turned on his heels, flew past me, through the door and up the stair. I flew up after him. Mr Bannerman opened Mr Lamb's door.'

'Where was Mr Lamb at this time?'

'Mr Lamb was standing just in front of him, immediately inside the door. Mr Bannerman said to him, "Was that insult to me, Lamb?". Mr Lamb did not answer, but I noticed he was holding a cutlass in his right hand and the sheath in his left.'

'Now, this is a most important point, Miss Young, where was the weapon pointed?'

'The cutlass and the sheath were pointing upwards.'

'Thank you, please continue, Miss Young.'

'Then, Mr Bannerman grabbed Mr Lamb's wrists. Mr Lamb wasn't trying to use the cutlass, though. The men struggled to the middle of the bedroom with the cutlass. I went in between them and tried to separate them. The cutlass was pointing upwards at that time, but it fell slightly on my right hand and it gave me a cut. I said at that time, "Oh, it has cut me!". Then Mr Bannerman became even more furious to get the cutlass from Mr Lamb's hand, and they struggled over to the fireplace.'

'Miss Young, after you noticed that your hand was cut, what happened next?'

'I was rubbing my hand. The next thing I heard was Mr Bannerman saying, "Oh, I am wounded. Send for a doctor." I don't know if the cutlass was still in Mr Lamb's hand, at that time, though.'

'And how where the two men positioned?'

'Mr Bannerman was standing at the fireplace with his left leg inside the fender. Mr Lamb was facing him.'

'Did you see the accused man stab Bannerman?'

'I did not.'

Robert MacGregor Mitchell objected on behalf of the defence at this juncture:

'Objection, your honour. Miss Young, on the night of Mr Lamb's arrest, did you not say to Constable Pritchard that you *actually witnessed* Lamb stab Mr Bannerman with the cutlass?'

'Yes.'

'And did you, in fact, even demonstrate how it was done?'

'I did.'

'And why did you say that Lamb had stabbed Bannerman, if you now say you did not actually see that happen?'

'Because I had concluded that he had done so. I was in a very agitated state at the time, and did not know rightly what I was saying.'

The next witness for the Crown, Mrs Janet Bannerman, the widow of the deceased man, testified that:

'My husband left the house on the Sunday night in question about seven o'clock. He did not tell me where he was going, and I did not see him alive again. I also did not know Miss Young, nor did I know that my husband visited her.'

Dr Robert Menzies presented the post-mortem evidence, and expressed the opinion that:

'The wound from which the deceased died was approximately four inches in depth and one inch wide, and had been made by a forcible thrust from a sharp instrument. It was found to have almost completely severed the femoral artery. Death was due to acute arterial haemorrhage.

The nature of the wound precludes me from giving a definite opinion as to whether it had been inflicted intentionally or accidentally. The wound was horizontal and its infliction must have required some force. Tests on the lower five inches of the blade showed the presence of human blood. There were no other injuries to the victim's body, and no signs of a struggle except for the cut on Miss Young's hand.'

That ended the lacklustre case presented by the prosecution. It was now time for Robert MacGregor Mitchell KC to present the case for the defence. Mitchell announced that he would not be calling Charles Lamb to testify, but did paint an eloquent picture of the accused man to the jury,

'A quiet, peaceful man, who was teetotal. He was a steady workman who was kind and patient, he had lodged at Miss Young's house in Canal Crescent for nineteen years. He was pleasant and helped care for Miss Young's nephew on occasion. Mr Lamb, who had grown fond of Miss Young over the years clearly objected to William Bannerman, a married man, developing a friendship with his landlady. Mr Bannerman, on the other hand, twenty-five years Lamb's Junior, had not taken into account the older man's size and strength. Lamb had previously been both a footballer and a boxer.'

Despite only calling two character witnesses for the defence (who described Charles Lamb as 'A good-living, kind-hearted and respectable man), Robert MacGregor Mitchell KC had researched his defence thoroughly. He revealed to the court that William Bannerman had previously threatened to 'Give the old man a good shaking. It would do him no harm.'

Mr Mitchell also claimed that Charles Lamb remembered warning Bannerman during the struggle, 'Watch, you'll cut yourself. It's sharp!'" Although Miss Young did not remember this.

He brought the defence's case to a close, reminding the jury that:

'Should you choose to imprison a sixty-five-year-old man here, he will most likely spend the rest of his natural life in prison.'

Lord Moncrieff then summed up the case for the jury, 'Members of the jury, no doubt Lamb objected to the frequent resort of Bannerman to the company of a maiden lady by a married man. Bannerman apparently knew this, for he had said the old man would be none the worse in his old age of severe shaking. On the other hand, Lamb on the evening in question, had certainly used provocative words, and accordingly struck the match.

Up to this point, Charles Lamb had not suggested an attack on Bannerman. When Bannerman opened the door of Lamb's bedroom, the accused had the weapon pointing upwards, that is not the posture which a man takes when proposing to use a cutlass either for attack or defence. Lamb continued in that position until Bannerman stepped forward and caught Lamb by the wrist. One would have thought that if Lamb proposed to use the cutlass that would have been the time to make a thrust or a sweep.

The cut sustained by Miss Young seems to have been caused by the motion of the cutlass, which Lamb would not have made if he had been able to control its movement. I believe, as he was on the most friendly of terms with Miss Young, he had not designed to give her a slash with the weapon.

There are two theories in this case. The theory of the Crown is that during the struggle Lamb altered his tactics, and instead of merely resisting, struck an aggressive blow. This theory suggests that Bannerman was standing with his legs apart, forcing the wrists of Lamb downwards, and it was Bannerman's object to pull the cutlass towards the ground, so to avoid doing himself injury, and yet be able to master his opponent. At this point, the Crown suggests, Lamb chose to become the aggressor and to stab Bannerman.

The theory of the defence, on the other hand, is that during the course of the struggle the weapon's point was diverted by Bannerman to an extent for which Lamb was not responsible.'

Lord Moncrieff then directed the jury to disregard much of the evidence given to the police by Miss Williamina Young immediately after the incident, and remarked:

'A certain touch of tragedy attaches itself to Miss Young in this matter. She was in a condition of almost daughterly affection with Mr Lamb. She was also in the embarrassing position of having a perfectly honourable affection for a man whom she could not marry, and I think she gave a very admirable picture of integrity and character in the statement that she made.'

Lord Moncrieff then instructed the jury to retire and debate whether Charles Lamb was guilty of culpable homicide in the death of William Bannerman.

Charles Lamb, who had stood calmly throughout the trial,

sporting long side whiskers and an expensive tweed suit, did not have to wait long to learn his fate. In perhaps the quickest verdict in the history of Perth High Court, the jury debated their decision for only one minute. Their unanimous verdict of 'not guilty' was accompanied in the crowded courtroom by a cacophony of loud clapping and cheering. After being dismissed by Lord Moncrieff 'without a stain upon your character', Charles Lamb left the court a free man. A large crowd outside jostled to shake his hand and congratulate him as he was bundled quickly away.

He returned to Canal Crescent and lived out his remaining years, before passing away suddenly on 24 April 1938. His funeral took place at a packed Dunkeld Cathedral a few days later.

This bizarre trial remains one of the strangest in the rich history of the High Court in Perth. Four important questions remain unanswered, which do not appear to have been probably addressed during the proceedings.

Firstly, the personal relationship between the three protagonists in this strange affair was never properly questioned, by either side. Indeed, Charles Lamb was not even asked to testify. Secondly, Lord Moncrieff seemed far more concerned in praising Miss Young for her bravery, than in examining the validity of her evidence. The entire case seems to have been decided on the evidence of one witness, without any corroboration. Thirdly, if the death of William Bannerman was entirely accidental, as the verdict implies, with no aggressive intention or premeditation on Lamb's behalf, why was he already holding the unsheathed cutlass in his hand *before* Bannerman had even entered the room?

Finally, there is one intriguing question which, depending on the answer, may have had some bearing on the outcome of the case. How, why, and when did a 65-year-old painter from Dunkeld come to be in possession of an exotic nineteenth-century cutlass in the first place?

17 – THE PAPER TOWN KILLER
(Part One)

The evening of Sunday, 8 May 1960 was much the same as any other in the community of Leslie, on the outskirts of Glenrothes. Men drank in the pubs and working men's clubs, before wandering home to prepare for the following day's shift at the Fettykil Paper Mill or at the Fife collieries, while their wives and families attended a screening of *Kidnapped* at the Regal Cinema.

Two men, Alexander McCrorie, aged 28, and Hugh Friel, 25, had spent most of that day drinking at Rothes Memorial Club, the Miners' Institute and the Ex-Servicemen's Club in the nearby village of Kinglassie. After a drunken singsong the two men left the Miners' Institute at 10.30pm. A witness would later report that both men seemed to be 'greatly affected by drink, Friel especially so. But they were on friendly terms.'

Both McCrorie and Friel lived in Leslie and had known each other for many years. After working away in High Wycombe for a month, McCrorie had recently returned to Leslie to resume his employment at the local paper mill,

while Friel worked at one of the Fife collieries.

They obtained a lift back to Leslie from Kinglassie in a friend's car, and were dropped off at the junction of North Street and the High Street. At this point there appears to have been some disagreement among the two men and a fist fight ensued. McCrorie then stepped away from the fracas, as if to end it or perhaps to draw breath. However, instead of returning to his wife and children in Main Street, he chased after Friel, who by now had continued walking towards his own home in Kirk Drive, a few hundred yards to the northeast.

Around 11.15pm, householders in Rothes Park overheard the sound of two raised male voices in the street outside, accompanied by a scuffle, followed by what appeared to be the noise of footsteps running away. Several residents were roused from their beds and opened the curtains, but could see nothing immediately. Nineteen-year-old John Coughlin happened to be staying with friends at number 36 Rothes Park and alarmed by the disturbance, went outside into the street. Number 36 was adjacent to an alleyway leading to a cul-de-sac of houses known as Mount Pleasant. In 1960, these houses stood next to an open area of land known as Prinlaws (on which Leslie Primary School now stands). On coming out of the house, John Coughlin immediately noticed Hugh Friel lying on the roadway, close to the alleyway entrance. Friel's motionless body was partially illuminated by the almost full moon and the dim streetlights. His face and head were covered in blood, rendering him almost unrecognisable. As a crowd gathered, the police and ambulance services were quickly summoned to attend to the badly injured man.

In the meantime, McCrorie appeared at his parent's door at 50 Lomond View. It was now approximately 11.45pm. He was now accompanied by his wife, Margaret, who was pushing a pram, and their pet dog. His sister was still awake and answered the door, wondering why someone would be calling so late at night.

Seeing blood on her brother's hands and clothes she asked,

'What's wrong?'

'I've been fighting, I think I've killed a man,' McCrorie replied, 'I hit him with an axe.'

Before he left his parent's house, McCrorie changed his clothes and washed his hands. He then left his bloodstained clothes behind, together with an axe-head which had been concealed in his jacket pocket. Before leaving with his wife, he turned and said to his sister, 'I'm going to give myself up.'

Fifteen minutes later, around midnight, John Coughlin, the witness who had first seen Hugh Friel's body, noticed a couple appear from the alleyway onto Rothes Park. He recognised them as Alexander McCrorie and wife, Margaret. She was still pushing a pram.

'Who's the injured man?' McCrorie asked John Coughlin, 'I might know him.'

'I don't know,' replied Coughlin.

McCrorie attempted to push through the crowd, for a better view, but was told to move on by the police officer. He then walked past the scene with his wife before disappearing from view. Meanwhile, despite the best efforts of the medical staff, Hugh Friel died en route to hospital. He was pronounced dead in the ambulance at 12.25am. An immediate murder investigation was launched.

Alexander McCrorie did not have time to give himself up, as he had promised. Early on Monday morning, just a few hours after the attack of Hugh Friel had taken place, he was arrested at his home in Leslie by Police Constable Archibald Smith. After being charged and having his rights read to him, McCrorie told PC Smith, 'Friel had been with my wife. He told me. Now I have to tell you. I don't want to save myself. It was an axe-head I used. I left it at my mother's.'

McCrorie appeared handcuffed to a CID officer at his preliminary hearing in Cupar. He was informed that Wednesday, 27 July 1960 had been set as the date of his murder trial. The High Court in Perth would be the venue.

When the day of the trial finally arrived, there was intense interest in Perth. A large throng gathered both in the public gallery and outside while McCrorie was escorted silently into the court. Lord Guest presided as the jury of eight men and seven women was chosen. The charge was then read out:

'Alexander Gardner McCrorie, you are charged that you did on May 8th, 1960, assault Hugh Berry Friel in Rothes Park, Leslie, by striking him repeatedly on the head and face with an axe-head or similar instrument, and did murder him. How do you plead?'

To the court's surprise, the accused man replied, 'not guilty.'

The prosecution produced a stream of witnesses who testified that McCrorie and Friel had spent Sunday afternoon and evening together drinking. One witness estimated that McCrorie had 'drunk twenty pints of beer.'

Next came the medical evidence. The post-mortem results confirmed that Hugo Friel had died as a result of several blows to the head and face, with the doctor stating that, 'Despite knowing the deceased for several years, I was unable to recognise him, due the severity of the injuries to his face.'

The prosecution then produced twelve witnesses to confirm that McCrorie had been in Friel's company on the night of his death. Coupled with the murder weapon – which contained the accused man's thumbprint, and the statement already given by McCrorie to the police, the Crown rested its case.

J A Forsyth QC, McCrorie's defence counsel, did not call a single witness. Instead, he informed the court that he intended to place the accused man on the stand. Including the prosecution's cross-examination, McCrorie would be grilled for more than two hours.

'Mr McCrorie, please explain to the court what happened that night,' Mr Forsyth began.

'Yes Sir. I am Alexander McCrorie. I am married with two children, aged four and eighteen months. I have known Hugh Friel all my life and had always been on good terms with him. But that night he goaded me into a fight by starting an argument.'

'What was the argument that Friel started?' asked Mr Forsyth.

'He claimed that he had been carrying on with my wife, Meg, and sleeping with her while I was working in England. He said, "She's no' bad, is she?" We come to blows with our fists as we came out of North Street, and I decided to go home and ask Meg if it was true or not. All the time Friel was behind me shouting, "Go on then! Ask and find out!" But on the way, I realised that it must have been a parcel of lies, as my wife had been staying with my mother while I was working away.

I decided that I wanted to teach Friel a lesson for slandering Meg. Instead of going into the house, I went into the coal shed to get a stick or something to even the fight up. Friel was more than a match for me with his fists.'

'Can you explain this remark, please, Mr McCrorie,' his advocate interjected.

'Yes,' the accused man answered, 'my left arm is weak. I've not had the proper use of the shoulder muscle for my left arm through an accident at birth.'

'Thank you. Please continue.'

'I couldn't find a stick, but I came across an axe-head, which I lifted up and put in my pocket. I followed Friel and caught up with him again on the street.'

'Was there a further conversation there?' enquired Mr Forsyth.

'He started the same thing again, about my wife, sneering and jeering at me. He was trying to get my temper, I suppose. He said, "Have you asked her the truth?", and I said that I had not. We fought again with our firsts along the length of the street, then Friel started to run. That is when I used the axe-head. I ran after him and, at the end of the path leading to a cul-de-sac, I struck him on the side of the face with it. There is a step down and he stumbled and fell. He must have hit his head on the ground. I lost my head. I must have struck him again with the axe-head, but I don't remember doing it.'

'Why did you want to teach him a lesson so badly?'

'He maybe could have said the same thing about the wife of someone else up the street.'

'Thank you, Mr McCrorie, no further questions.'

Under cross-examination by the prosecution, McCrorie admitted that he 'had been wild and in a temper with Friel' but added that 'I had never been afraid of him or in fear that my own life was in danger.'

With that, the questioning of the accused man was completed.

In their final addresses, both counsels reminded the jury of their obligations. The prosecution reinforced the violence of the assault on Mr Friel and the element of premeditation introduced into the case when the defendant chose to return home and – instead of retiring to his bed to lick his wounds – chose instead to fetch an axe-head, with which he blatantly intended to return to the street and complete his attack on the victim. The Crown considered that the ferocity of the attack alone warranted nothing other than a verdict of wilful murder to be brought in against the accused man. In addition, the jury were reminded that, 'the court had only Mr McCrorie's word that Friel had made the allegations regarding his wife, since there were no other witnesses to this accusation.'

Mr Forsyth, for the defence, then reminded the jury that the accused man 'had never intended to kill Mr Friel, just to "even up the fight", due to his weaker left arm. In addition, the mitigating circumstances brought about by the upsetting allegations regarding the defendant's wife, and the large amount of liquor he had consumed, had no doubt clouded Mr McCrorie's judgement and brought about a temporary change in his behaviour. These extreme circumstances, I believe, do not warrant a verdict of murder in this case, but some lesser verdict which truly reflects all the circumstances detailed here.'

Lord Guest then gave his final summation, reminding the jury members of the grave nature of the assault, before instructing the fifteen jurors to retire and consider their verdict.

After an absence of 34 minutes the jury returned.

'Members of the jury, have you reached in this case?'

'Yes. We find the defendant not guilty of murder, but guilty of culpable homicide.'

There was a palpable murmur of astonishment in the public gallery and from the front bench.

Culpable homicide is defined under Scottish law as 'the killing of a person in circumstances which are neither accidental nor justified, but where the wicked intent to kill or wicked recklessness required for murder is absent.' Although there is no verdict of manslaughter in Scottish courts, unlike in England, culpable homicide is the approximate equivalent.

The verdict was a unanimous one, although Lord Guest was clearly surprised at the Jury's leniency in their decision. Interestingly, even if the accused man been found guilty of murder, recent changes in the law would have almost certainly meant McCrorie being found guilty of a 'non-capital' murder, rather than a capital offence, and therefore avoiding the death penalty.

By the mid-1950s growing public distaste for the death penalty had led to a revision on the statute books in both English and Scottish Law. Despite *The Gower Report* in 1953 recommending the retention of the death penalty in all cases of murder, lobbying continued, resulting in The Homicide Act 1957. On conviction for murder, hanging was now restricted to a list of particular circumstances such as killing another person during a robbery, by shooting, in an explosion, or for the murder of a police or prison officer. All other murders would now carry a mandatory penalty of life imprisonment. There had been no execution at Perth Prison since 1948. The circumstances of this tragic case, it seems, did not warrant a further one.

Lord Guest then addressed the court:

'Although the jury has been able to take a merciful view in this case, I cannot regard the prisoner's brutal attack upon the deceased as anything other than a crime of extreme seriousness. You will go to prison for fifteen years. Take the prisoner away.'

McCrorie appeared to be resigned to the verdict. However,

his wife broke down in tears as the sentence was passed and was led away sobbing. Before McCrorie was taken away to begin his sentence, his wife was allowed to see him in the adjacent courtroom cells for a few minutes, in the presence of his defence counsel. Following the conclusion of that short meeting Mr Forsyth announced that he would launch an immediate appeal against the verdict.

The Court of Criminal Appeal in Edinburgh heard McCrorie's appeal two months later, on Tuesday, 4 October 1960. The convicted man's legal team laboured furiously, angered by the perceived harshness of the fifteen-year sentence imposed at the High Court in Perth. McCrorie's solicitor employed the high-profile and colourful advocate Nicholas Fairbairn QC to argue his case at the appeal hearing. Fairbairn would later become a Member of Parliament, Solicitor General for Scotland and receive a knighthood.

Fairbairn argued that McCrorie had acted under extreme provocation, out of character and only as a last resort, after Friel had boasted of committing adultery with McCrorie's wife. 'McCrorie had become so enraged at this,' Fairbairn insisted, 'that he struck Hugh Friel and killed him.'

Fairbairn then argued to the appeal judges that:

'At the original trial Lord Guest, in imposing the harsh sentence of fifteen years, had neglected the attitude of the jury that there had been strong provocation in McCrorie's actions.'

Nevertheless, on considering these grounds, the appeal judges unanimously agreed that they could not interfere with the original sentence imposed. McCrorie was taken back to Barlinnie Prison in Glasgow to complete the remainder of his fifteen-year term.

And there the story of 'The Paper Town Killer', as one newspaper had dubbed McCrorie, seemed to be over. Sadly, though, the death of Hugh Friel would prove to be merely act one of this intense drama. Act two would also be played out at the High Court in Perth.

18 – THE PAPER TOWN KILLER
(Part Two)

With Alexander McCrorie now languishing in Barlinnie Prison, following his failed appeal, those affected by the killing of Hugh Friel were left to pick up the pieces. McCrorie's two young children remained with his wife Margaret at the family's home in Leslie.

Within two years McCrorie's family circumstances had dramatically changed. By spring 1962 Margaret had begun a relationship with another man, Russell Miln, and began divorce proceeding against her husband. From behind bars McCrorie blocked the proceedings. Margaret had informed her new lover that she was single. Blissfully unaware, he then proposed marriage. As a result, a bigamous wedding took place between the couple at Townhead Church in Royston Hill, Glasgow on 14 July 1962. However, almost before the ink was dry on their marriage certificate, news of the nuptials reached McCrorie's family and Margaret was forced to confess. She walked into a Glasgow Police Station two weeks after her wedding day and admitted committing bigamy. After an appearance at Glasgow Sheriff's Court in August she was fined £10 (approximately £260 today). Margaret, in mitigation, told the magistrates that McCrorie had blocked her attempts to seek a divorce, and she still hoped to be a free woman as soon as possible.

Meanwhile, shocked by the news that his marriage had survived less than two years of his fifteen-year incarceration, McCrorie began divorce proceedings of his own, as he resigned himself to the remainder of his term inside.

Another six years would pass until, in the autumn of 1968, Alexander McCrorie was granted parole on licence from prison, as a result of his good behaviour while imprisoned. His early release caused some understandable disquiet in Leslie. Nevertheless, he returned to his hometown and set about rebuilding his life. Before long he gained employment at the paper mill and became a fixture again at the local pubs and working men's clubs. He does not appear to have made any attempt at a reconciliation with Margaret.

McCrorie quickly settled into a routine. He continued working at the paper mill, spending his free time walking his dog or drinking with friends and work colleagues. One workmate described him as, 'never without companions, he enjoyed a flutter, went drinking a lot and enjoyed the company of women.' Life in Leslie seemed to carry on much as before, until the morning of Friday, 24 October 1975 at an attractive end-of-terrace cottage in Leslie.

That Friday morning, Fife Police were summoned to number 11 Mansfield at 8.30am by Kate Stephen, who had called at the upstairs flat in the cottage to see her daughter Kathy before work. Kate Stephen found the door broken and ajar. Inside the flat, she discovered 42-year Kathy lying dead on the bedroom floor, in a bloodstained nightie. She had been stabbed 38 times.

Detective-Superintendents Tom Grieve and James Morgan from Fife Police took charge of the investigation, ordering a search of the Leslie and Glenrothes area. Initial assumptions were that Kathy Stephen had been killed during a robbery gone wrong. There had been three attempts to burgle Kathy's flat during the past year. Were the previous break-ins linked to her murder, police asked themselves? Kathy was the manager of the local betting shop in Douglas Road, and police conjectured that someone had expected to find large amounts of cash hidden inside her flat.

At a hastily arranged press conference, Detective-Superintendent Grieve spoke to the assembled reporters:

'Our officers are currently confining the search for Kathy Stephen's killer to the local area. We believe her murderer is a local man, or someone with extensive local knowledge, and probably acting alone. It is possible that someone in Leslie knows him and could be unwittingly shielding him. We will be knocking on every door in Leslie as part of this inquiry. A total of sixty CID and uniformed men are now involved in the manhunt, with about forty going round knocking on doors and the others checking gardens, fields, waste ground, and other areas for the murder weapon. In the meantime, we have removed several items from the property for examination.

The attack was a particularly savage one and we are interested in interviewing anyone who was out late on Thursday night or could not explain their absence from home.

If you noticed anyone or anything in the area of Mansfield between 11.30pm on Thursday and 2am yesterday, please contact the incident room at Glenrothes. Thank you.'

Questioning of every male resident in Leslie began. When police interviewed Alexander McCrorie on 28 October at his home, 27 Glenwood Road, they were no doubt already aware of his previous conviction. McCrorie could provide no alibi for the crucial time period; however, he did inform the police that he had been out walking and had bumped into another local man, David Millar, somewhere close to the scene of the murder. According to McCrorie's claim, Millar had informed him that 'something had happened to Kathy Stephen.' McCrorie also confessed to the officers that 'I should have told you earlier, but I didn't want to get involved', and 'I didn't do it, but I know who did.' This information immediately gave police David Millar as their prime suspect and he was brought in for questioning.

The interrogation of Millar did not last long, however. He was able to provide an ironclad alibi for the hours during which Kathy Stephen was thought to have been killed. Furthermore, he denied ever meeting McCrorie. So why had McCrorie been so keen to put David Millar 'in the frame'? The answer was a simple one – to divert suspicion from himself.

Under intense questioning by Fife CID detectives, McCrorie's answers were erratic. His version of events also varied enough for the police to be certain of his guilt. He appeared before Sheriff McInnes in Cupar on 23 January 1976 and was charged – for a second time in his life – with murder:

'Alexander Gardner McCrorie, you are charged that you did, on October 24th last year, in the dwelling house at 11 Mansfield, Leslie, assault Katherine Amelia Stephen by striking her repeatedly about the head, body, and limbs with a knife or other similar instrument and thereby murdered her.'

McCrorie answered the charge with only the words 'not guilty.' He was then remanded in custody until 3 February when his murder trial would take place. Once again, the proceedings would take place at the High Court in Perth. Despite having only ten days between arraignment and trail, the Crown had already prepared their case thoroughly. It was announced that no less than 111 prosecution witnesses would be called. This time the authorities did not intend McCrorie to escape with anything less than a guilty verdict.

Ironically, Nicholas Fairbairn the once-libertarian advocate who, fifteen years earlier, had appealed for more leniency in McCrorie's first sentence had now become the Conservative MP for Kinross and Western Perthshire. He spent much of January and February 1976 sharing the newspaper headlines with McCrorie, arguing against everything from further spending on the arts, to decrying calls for increased rights for gay people.

Meanwhile, Alexander McCrorie was unlikely to have noticed the irony as he stood pensively in the dock at the High Court in Perth on 3 February. Lord Henry Keith stared sternly at him as the charge of murder was read aloud.

'How do you plead?'

'Not guilty,' came the reply from the prisoner. The Crown would need to prove McCrorie's guilt once again.

Advocate-Depute for Perthshire, Hugh Morton QC, began the prosecution's case with the aid of several witnesses who helped establish the chain of events on the tragic night in question. Kathy Stephen had spent the night before her death at her brother's pub, where she had taken part in a dominoes competition. She left to drive home at 12.45am; the last time she was seen alive. At 1.50am an elderly neighbour, Mr James Buchan, testified to hearing the sound of a woman screaming repeatedly. Alarmed, he looked out of his window, but could see nothing and returned to bed. He heard nothing else that night.

The victim's brother, Alexander Stephen, explained to the court that his sister normally took her betting shop takings home in a shopping bag. She had been advised against it, especially after previous burglary attempts at her home, but persisted in doing so.

Kathy Stephen's mother described calling at her daughter's flat around 8.30am the following morning only to find the front door lock broken and the door still ajar. This was followed by the medical evidence detailing the ferocity of the attack on Kathy. She had been stabbed 38 times and her time of decease was estimated to have been between 2am and 3am on the morning of 24 October.

Next came the shocking and damaging evidence given by Andrew Payne, a work colleague of McCrorie's. Payne testified that he had spent the evening before Kathy's death drinking and talking with the accused man. McCrorie told

Payne that he had visited Kathy Stephen's betting shop earlier that day and had lost about £15 (approximately £160 today). According to Payne's testimony, McCrorie had returned home with him, and the pair had continued drinking until around 1am, when McCrorie had left. The witness heard no more from the accused man until four days later when he had received a note from McCrorie in which he stated that he intended to take his own life. Payne then rushed to McCrorie's home in Glenwood Road, only to find the door barred. With some difficulty he managed to force his way inside, to find McCrorie collapsed on the floor, his wrists slashed, his arms covered in blood. He was rushed to hospital where the bleeding was staunched – although McCrorie's physical scars from his failed suicide attempt were still visible to all those in court.

It was now time for the defence to present their case. In a repeat of McCrorie's previous appearance at the Perth court, fifteen years earlier, no witnesses were called. Instead, his advocate, J S Forbes QC, placed McCrorie on the stand and proceeded to question him for more than two hours.

'Mr McCrorie, you have pled "not guilty" to this offence?'

'Yes, sir.'

'Then, can you please testify to this court exactly what did happen on the night in question.'

'On October 23rd,' McCrorie claimed, 'I left Andrew Payne's house about 10.30pm, after drinking with him. Then I went to another house in Hazel Place in Leslie, where I wanted to have sex with the woman living there. I didn't succeed and I left about 1am. I was walking down Mansfield on my way home when I bumped into Dave Millar hurrying out of a close at number 11. He told me "Something was wrong with Kathy" and we went into her house to see. The door was open, he went in first and I followed him. It was in darkness.'

'Were you directed to any room?' Mr Forbes enquired.

'Yes, Dave Millar said "that room there", and he pointed

straight to the bedroom in front,' McCrorie replied.

'What did you see?'

'I looked to the left and saw a figure between the two beds.'

'Did you do anything?'

'I went forward and sort of lifted Kathy up. She looked as if she'd been attacked and stabbed. I didn't know whether she was alive or dead. I didn't want to get involved so instead of dialling 999 for help, I used a piece of paper to wipe my fingerprints from a door handle and a light switch, before going home. There was a knife on the floor, so I picked it up and threw it in the burn. I must have got bloodstains on my suit and jersey when I lifted her, and a spot of blood on my shoes at the same time. A few hours later I burned them on a rubbish tip, because I didn't want to be implicated.'

Under cross-examination by the Advocate-Depute, Hugh Morton QC, McCrorie was reminded of the earlier testimony of Detective Inspector John Westland who had described the accused man's behaviour during police interrogation:

'Mr McCrorie, according to the testimony of the Inspector, you "became agitated during questioning, began swearing and went into a spasm. You shook uncontrollably and had to be supported in your seat." The Inspector added that you changed your story a number of times about why you burned your suit. May I also remind you that the police searched your house thoroughly and could find no trace of the grey suit and white polo neck jersey which witnesses said you had been wearing on the night.

In addition, the police interviewed Mr Millar, as a result of a statement given by you, but did not find anything to link him with the killing. In fact, in the words of Detective Inspector Westland, "Our investigations excluded everybody in Leslie except Alexander McCrorie".'

With that final blow landed by the prosecution, Lord Keith summed up the evidence and instructed the jury to consider their verdict. McCrorie's prior conviction had not been revealed to either Lord Keith, or to the jurors, during the course of the proceedings. Under Scottish law, at any trial in which the defendant has entered a verdict of not guilty, and during which, his previous good character has not been used as a tool by the defence, an accused person's previous convictions cannot be mentioned. However, if it is felt that any previous convictions might affect the severity of sentencing, a defendant's earlier criminal record can be reported to the judge – but only after the jury's verdict has been declared in court.

In Alexander McCrorie's case, any prior knowledge of his past offence would have surely heavily influenced the outcome of his trial. However, with the prosecution still needing to prove his guilt beyond reasonable doubt, perhaps McCrorie still hoped to walk from the court a free man. He would not have to wait long to learn his fate.

After just twenty minutes the jury returned with a unanimous verdict of guilty. McCrorie stood impassively as Advocate-Depute High Morton QC revealed the details of his 1960 conviction for culpable homicide. The Perth courtroom sat in a disbelieving silence as Lord Keith addressed McCrorie:

'Prisoner at the bar, you have heard the verdict of the jury. They have unanimously found you guilty of murder and the penalty for murder is fixed by law – it is imprisonment for life. Take him away.'

An additional charge of perjury seemed superfluous.

Kathy Stephen's mother wept openly as her daughter's murderer was escorted from the courtroom to be taken to Barlinnie Prison in Glasgow. On the steps of the courthouse David Millar, who had been wrongly accused of the murder, spoke to the waiting press:

'I'm glad it's all over now. I was actually in bed when McCrorie claimed he had met me in the street. These past three months have been a terrible time for me, with this allegation hanging over my head. Justice had now been done and I can get on with my life.'

McCrorie, then aged 44, would remain incarcerated until

he passed away at the age of 65, due to ill-health, in 1997. He had previously been refused parole.

His ex-wife Margaret continued to live in Leslie until her death in 2012 at the age of 80.

Conceivably, had the jury at McCrorie's first trial in 1960 not taken such a lenient approach, and had the parole board not seen fit to release him after only eight years served, the senseless death of Kathy Stephen fifteen years later would have almost certainly been avoided.

19 – SUICIDE OR MURDER?

December 1945 – Some of the many tragedies suffered during the Second World War were not felt until after the fighting had ceased. This is one such story, which bears an uncanny resemblance to the story of the murdered teashop waitress in my previous book *Perthshire's Pound of Flesh*.

Four days after Christmas 1945 the High Street in Kirkcaldy, Fife, was gradually returning to normality. Despite being the first Christmas since the end of hostilities, shortages were rife and the temperatures biting. In search of a warming cup of tea and a respite from the cold weather, many customers had sought refuge in the Rialto Tearooms at 188–190 High Street. The smell of baking drifted through the café from the small bakehouse at the rear.

The manageress, May Leslie, was twenty years of age and looked after the busy café with the help of two fifteen-year-old waitresses, Nola and Mary. The two young girls knew May to be a single woman who enjoyed going dancing, although they would soon discover that May Leslie led something of a double life.

Just after 2pm on that Saturday afternoon a young man, Donald MacLean Cameron, walked into the Rialto and paused a moment at the door, he appeared to be looking for someone. The two young waitresses both recognised Cameron. He was a shipyard worker at the Methil shipyard and was still dressed in his overalls. Although aged 25, Cameron had not been required to enlist in the army, as shipbuilding was a reserved occupation. In fact, he had moved from the Clyde shipyards a year earlier to take employment in Fife.

Nola and Mary were aware of a relationship between May, the Rialto's manageress, and the young shipyard worker, as Cameron often called at the café to visit her. On this occasion, however, he appeared pale and fraught. While the two girls were chatting to another customer, Cameron walked through to the small bakehouse at the rear of the café and motioned towards May to follow him.

Shortly afterwards, those in the café heard a woman scream, followed by the sound of two gunshots (approximately three seconds apart) coming from the rear of the café. Moments later, May Leslie staggered from the door at the side of the building, into the narrow close outside, then stumbled past the windows of the café and onto the High Street. Passersby turned in horror as May screamed 'Someone's shot me! I've been shot! Help!' before collapsing onto the cobbled street in front of the café. Shoppers ran to assist and a police constable was summoned. Another witness glanced into the narrow close at the side of the Rialto and noticed Donald Cameron emerge from the side door clutching his chest. He staggered briefly before slumping on the floor still holding his blood-soaked chest. An army service revolver fell from his hand onto the frosty ground.

May Leslie was carried inside the café while an ambulance was called. The Deputy Chief Constable, William Hunter, who was nearby, soon arrived on the scene. May was bleeding profusely from a gunshot wound to the abdomen, and the experienced Chief Constable instantly realised the seriousness of the injury.

'What is your name?' he asked.

'Mary Ann Heath.' the young manageress replied. The two young waitresses looked at each other in horror and surprise. They had always known her as May Leslie.

'What happened?' Deputy Chief Constable Hunter continued.

'I have been shot.'

'By whom?'

'Donald Cameron.'

While waiting for the ambulance to arrive, Donald Cameron – whose chest injury did not appear as serious – was taken in a patrol car to Kirkcaldy Police Station. After being medically examined he was taken into the charge room, where he was placed horizontally on a bench to be questioned later. A few minutes passed and Cameron seemed to recover somewhat. He then volunteered a statement to the constable stood by the door:

'Have I made it? I do not think I will. What are the chances of State aid? Did I shoot Mary through the stomach? Is she alright?'

The constable did not answer the young shipworker's enquiry. He had been ordered to remain silent.

Meanwhile, Mrs Mary Heath (as police officers soon discovered was May's real name and marital status) was rushed to Kirkcaldy General Hospital. Sadly, the extensive bleeding and damage to her organs proved too severe and she passed away the following morning. It was now a murder investigation.

Cameron was immediately arrested and, in the presence of his solicitor, was formally charged:

'Donald MacLean Cameron, you are accused of having, on December 29th 1945, in a close at 190 High Street, Kirkcaldy, assaulted Mary Ann Brown Leslie, or Heath, of 37 Victoria Road, Kirkcaldy, by discharging a loaded revolver at her and that you did injure her so severely that she died in

Kirkcaldy General Hospital the following day.'

Cameron entered a plea of 'not guilty' and his solicitor indicated that his client would be entering 'a plea of insanity at the earliest opportunity.' That 'earliest opportunity' would be a full five months later as the arrested man was then placed in confinement as an evaluation of his physical and mental health was ordered. Eventually, on 28th May 1946, Cameron's solicitor was granted the right to appear before Lord Cooper at the High Court in Perth to offer a special plea of insanity against the charge of murdering Mary Heath. Lord Cooper listened to the details of Cameron's mental condition but refused to entertain the request. The accused man was ordered back to his cell at Perth Prison and a trial date was set for Tuesday 11th June.

The trial opened at the High Court on Tay Street in Perth with queues quickly forming outside, as members of the public jostled for the few remaining seats in the public gallery. A high-profile judge had been appointed to oversee the trial. Sir David King Murray had served as the Solicitor General for Scotland as part of Churchill's wartime coalition government, and had recently been given the title 'The Honourable Lord Birnam'.

Cameron, represented by George Montgomery KC again pled 'not guilty' before the hushed courtroom. Sinclair Shaw, the Advocate-Depute, then began the case for the prosecution by calling the first witness, one of the young waitresses from the Rialto Tearooms.

'Please state your name for the court.'

The nervous witness, still only fifteen years of age, spoke in a quiet voice as she gave her evidence, 'Yes, sir. I am Nola Joan Ritchie of 10 Nicoll Street, Kirkcaldy. The dead woman, who was the manageress of the Rialto. was known to me as May Leslie, and it was not until much later that I was aware she was a married woman. After returning from my lunch on the day of the shooting, I saw Donald Cameron go into the bakehouse at the back. He was in his working clothes.'

'Did you recognise him, Miss Ritchie?' Mr Shaw enquired.

'Yes. He came in about once a week to see her, but he looked paler than usual on that day. While I was speaking to another customer in the shop, May Leslie, sorry, I mean Mrs Heath, went out to the back. Then a few moments later, I heard two shots and then screams coming from the bakehouse. Mrs Heath ran out of the close at the side onto the pavement out front shouting, "Somebody has shot me", then she collapsed.'

The next witness, Mary Smith Forbes, the other young waitress, explained what happened next:

'I saw her stagger past the café window shouting, "I am shot. He has shot me." I ran into the bakehouse at the back to see what had happened and I opened the side door. Donald Cameron was slumped against the wall in the passage.'

Joseph Heath, the 22-year-old husband that Mary had hidden from her colleagues at work, was the next witness to be called. His outward emotion was obvious to all in the courtroom. Within the space of just a few weeks, he had learned of his wife's death, her adultery and her denial of their relationship.

'Mr Heath, please explain, for the court, the background to your relationship with your wife and the accused man.'

'Yes,' replied the witness, fighting back tears as he testified, 'I am Joseph Heath of 19 Stewart Street, Dysart, husband of Mary. We were married in September 1943, but I had joined the army back in February of that year. After training, I was shipped abroad in October, a few weeks after our wedding. Then I started receiving letters from my family at home telling me that my wife was friendly with Cameron. When I was demobbed and returned home, I sought advice through the Legal Aid section of the army. They advised me to go and see her and talk to her, which I did. We were then reconciled.'

'And what happened then, Mr Heath?'

'Well, Sir, a few weeks before the shooting I was out walking with my wife when we met Cameron in the street. While I was talking with Cameron, trying to sort things out, my wife slapped his face.

Then, on the night before he shot her, me and my wife quarrelled over going to a dance, because I thought she meant to meet Cameron there. I slapped her on the face and she retaliated. Then she ran out of the house, shouting that she was going to do something to herself. I gave chase and brought her back, and afterwards we made up.'

'Thank you, Mr Heath. One final question. Where were you at the time of the shooting?'

'I was at a football match, sir.'

Next, William Hunter, the Deputy Chief Constable for Fife, took his place in the witness box. He confirmed that Donald Cameron has been found lying in the close to the side of the Rialto Tearooms and that he had sustained a gunshot wound to the chest, from which he had now recovered. Next to Cameron's body the police had found a recently fired service revolver containing four live and two spent cartridges.

The medical evidence – usually so decisive in murder cases – proved to be problematic for both the Crown and the defence. Four expert witnesses had been instructed by the court to examine and observe Donald Cameron during his incarceration in the Criminal Lunacy Wing at Perth Prison. Two psychiatric doctors gave the opinion that Cameron was sane and fit to face trial, while the remaining two testified that the accused man was insane at the time of the shooting, and therefore unable to stand trial for murder. Even the forensic evidence failed to provide anything in the way of concrete proof for either side. The ballistics experts at the police crime laboratory were only able to confirm that the shot that killed Mrs Heath had been discharged from less than 6 feet away, and that the bullet which entered Donald Cameron's chest had been fired from no further than 3 inches from its target. It was also impossible to state whether the gun had gone off accidentally or not.

With the evidence for the prosecution completed, it was now time for the defence. George Montgomery KC called only one witness (compared to the 31 called by the Crown), the accused man himself, Donald Cameron.

'Mr Cameron,' Montgomery began, 'please state for the court exactly what happened.'

'Yes, Sir. Well, I first met Mrs Heath at a dance at the end of 1944. I lived with her while her husband was away in the services. She told me she was expecting a baby at Christmas, but that she couldn't see me anymore, even though the baby was mine, and that she was going back to her husband. I made up my mind to commit suicide on December 29th 1945, and I called at the Rialto where I knew Mrs Heath worked on that day.'

'Why did you decide to commit suicide?'

'Because I was very depressed. She no longer wanted me, and my father had a rather Victorian attitude to my association with her. I tried talking to her in the bakehouse at the back of the shop, but she said she wouldn't change her mind. I took out the revolver and was about to turn it on myself when it went off accidently and hit her.'

In cross-examination, Shaw, the Advocate-Depute, pushed Donald Cameron on the conversation between the couple:

'Tell me, Mr Cameron, did you, in fact, quarrel with Mrs Heath because she had returned to her husband?'

George Montgomery, it seems, was well prepared for this line of attack by the Crown and had arranged for Cameron to demonstrate and clarify to the court exactly how he had pulled the revolver from his pocket and fired the deadly shot in error:

'I pulled the gun from my pocket like this,' he explained, 'and it went off accidentally as I swung it round to shoot myself. Realising what I'd done, I turned the revolver and shot myself. I loved that girl, the last thing I wanted to do was to injure her. I wanted to shoot myself.'

With this dramatic demonstration concluded, and with Cameron having given evidence for almost an hour, the defence rested their case leaving Lord Birnam the task of providing the jury of ten men and five women with his summation of the case:

'Ladies and gentlemen of the jury, two mental specialists have testified that Cameron was insane at the time of the shooting, while two others have asserted that Cameron was sane and fit to plead. I also remind you that some doctors believe that all criminals – to some degree or other – exhibit a degree of insanity when committing their crimes. However, members of the jury, you are charged here with administering the law as the law is; and not as these medical men would like it to be.'

The fifteen jurors duly retired to consider their verdict while Donald Cameron was led back to his cell to await his fate.

After 45 minutes the jury returned. Their verdict was a unanimous one. Guilty of murder. No plea for clemency was forthcoming from the jury and Lord Birnam donned his black cap before pronouncing the death penalty. Donald Cameron would be executed at Perth Prison on 9th July. Despite the severity of the ruling Cameron remained calm throughout the trial and onlookers even noticed a wry smile on his face as the death sentence was passed.

An immediate appeal was lodged by George Montgomery KC, which was heard at the Criminal Court of Appeal in Edinburgh on 4th July – just five days before Cameron's planned execution. In the immediate post-war years there was a great deal of public sympathy for returning soldiers whose wives had conducted affairs while their husbands had been risking their lives 'For King and Country'. The authorities, on the other hand, were dismayed at the rapid rise in gun-related crime, caused by the return of so many psychologically damaged servicemen, many of whom had failed to hand in their service weapons. While public distaste for the death penalty had increased, the establishment, on the other hand, saw that ultimate sanction as the only viable deterrent against the rising number of armed robberies and shootings.

George Montgomery based his appeal on three grounds. Firstly, that the presiding judge had failed to instruct the jury that 'they must be satisfied in reaching their verdict that the accused discharged the revolver either with intent to kill or recklessly, and with indifference as to whether death resulted or not.' Secondly, on the grounds that the judge failed to present to the jury the possible alternative verdict of 'guilty of culpable homicide', and finally, that there was 'no conclusive evidence from which it could competently be inferred that the accused discharged the revolver with criminal intent.'

However, despite the seemingly strong grounds for the appeal and the large petition for mercy which had been gathered, the court unanimously refused the appeal. The Lord Justice-General, Lord Normand, declared:

'The evidence was amply sufficient to justify the verdict of guilty of murder. This is not a case in which a possible verdict of culpable homicide, would have been inconsistent with the evidence.'

There would be no successful appeal for Donald Cameron. Agonisingly, however, as a result of the lengthy appeals process, the date of his execution was now pushed back to 22nd July.

Nevertheless, Cameron's supporters did not give up. A protest was made directly to the Secretary of State for Scotland, together with a 12,000-signature petition. Eventually, just three days before his planned appointment with the hangman, Cameron was granted a last-minute reprieve. His sentence was commuted to one of penal servitude for life. It had now been 38 years since Perth Prison had witnessed an execution. There would be just one more before the death penalty was finally abolished (the story of which is also featured in this book).

Mary Heath was buried quietly in her hometown a few days after her death.

Donald Cameron served his sentence and was released in the 1960s. He never revisited Kirkcaldy, but instead returned to the West of Scotland before passing away in Kilmarnock in 1984 at the age of 63.

20 – THE BRACO MURDER
(Part One – The Manhunt)

December 1869 – Around 8.30am on the morning of Wednesday, 22 December 1869, a special messenger arrived at Dunblane Police Station with information that a 64-year-old man named John Miller, who lived in the lonely Blackhill Tollhouse on the Glenlichorn Road, a mile north of Braco in the western stretches of Perthshire, had been found murdered at his home. According to the messenger, Miller, who lived alone in the tiny, two-room tollhouse, was last seen alive shortly before 9pm on the previous evening. He appeared to have been cooking his supper when the perpetrator, or perpetrators, of the deed entered his house, beat him savagely about the head, face and body, with a crowbar, ransacked the property for money and valuables, before escaping, leaving the old man dead. An immediate investigation was launched.

It was a frosty, inhospitable and gloomy morning as police officers arrived at Blackhill Tollhouse hoping to piece together the chain of events leading to John Miller's brutal killing. Although once married, John Miller had lived alone for several years in a frugal manner, cooking for himself and leading a generally solitary existence. Nevertheless, he was genial and occasionally received visits from friends. Miller was last seen alive between 8pm and 9pm on the previous evening, when a shepherd named Walter Maclaren had called in on his return journey to Muthill. Around 9pm Miller had waved goodbye at the door as Maclaren left, remarking to his visitor:

'I won't be late in going to my bed tonight, Walter.'

John Miller also advised his visitor to watch out for his dogs, as he had been warned that a 'big stout tramp' with a 'black-like' face had seen hanging around the fields.

No one – with the exception of his killer – would see John Miller alive again.

At 6.30am the following morning, a passing ploughman, Peter McLeish, who had intended to leave a bundle of clothes with John Miller, knocked on the door. He received no answer, so tried the handle and the windows only to find them fastened. At this point Mr Archibald McLaren, a miller from Blackhill, happened to be passing and both men hammered in vain on the door but received no answer.

Mary Bayne, John Miller's sister, lived a mile away at Ardoch and a message was sent instructing her to come quickly. On her arrival a pane of glass was cut from one of the tollhouse windows and the shutters burst open with an axe. Archibald McLaren entered first, only to reel back in horror at the sight that greeted him.

Inside the cramped and darkened room lay the corpse of the tollman, lying on his back in a pool of congealed blood. His head was facing the bed and his legs were spread in a contorted fashion across the floor. It appeared that the murderer had crept up behind the victim and beat him savagely with a crowbar which had been propped up inside the door. The instrument was still on the floor beside Miller's body, clotted with hair and blood. It was concluded that the old man had been cooking his supper (as a pan with some ham in it was found in the exhausted fire, and some bread and cheese had been laid out on the table). The murderer, who may have already been waiting inside the house, appeared to have felled John Miller with one hefty blow, then rained down a series of repeated blows until he was sure his victim was dead. He had then proceeded to plunder the house only to discover to his disappointment that Miller lived frugally and kept little of any value in the tollhouse.

The house had been ransacked but, with the exception of twenty shillings and a silver watch, the killer had uncovered little of value. However, it was at this moment that a gruesome discovery was made. Presumably covered in his victim's blood, the murderer had hit upon the idea of stealing the dead man's clothes to aid his getaway. Missing from the small wardrobe in the tollhouse was John Miller's 'Sunday best' – it seemed that cold-hearted killer had coolly dressed himself in the murdered man's clothes, leaving his own bloodstained and dirty attire on the floor. He had then left the tollhouse, locking the door and windows first, then throwing the key into the dung heap outside.

Ironically, the murderer's callous plan to avoid detection would have the opposite effect. The Perthshire Police compiled a complete list of both the stolen clothing and the items left behind by the killer. It would prove to be his undoing. The stolen clothes would eventually lead the authorities directly to the wanted man.

'CARRIED OFF FROM MR MILLER'S

A shooting coat and vest of dark fancy tweed, having a very small red heather-coloured thread in it; two outside pockets with large flaps and black composition buttons; a pair of coarse grey tweed trousers lined with twilled cotton, moleskin pockets, very little worn, and a watch-pocket supposed to have been sewed in by the deceased, a scarlet and black-checked woollen shirt, two white cotton shirts, and a pair of Blucher boots, plain soled; a silver pocket watch, jewelled in two holes, without maker's name or number, having a well-worn steel fob chain about four inches long with a brass key attached.

LEFT BEHIND

A sack coat, a vest, a pair of cotton-corded trousers, a short blue woollen shirt, an old pair of navvies' boots, and a pair of stockings.'

A description of the clothes was then distributed to every police station. Meanwhile, some local speculation came to the attention of Police Superintendent Peter Stewart. Firstly, it had long been rumoured that John Miller kept a large amount of cash at the tollhouse and, secondly, three vagrants, had been seen near Braco in recent days. Even more alarmingly, Miller's nephew reported seeing:

'A big stout black-like man' who had spoken to his uncle outside the tollhouse, on the day before his death. This mysterious stranger had lit a pipe, then 'walked backward and forward before the tollhouse for some time, carrying a gun. But what became of the man, after I left, I do not know. I supposed him to be a game-watcher at Ardoch. I had never seen this man before. My uncle said he seemed to be well acquainted with the railways, as he talked a lot about the porters there.'

It was conjectured that the man may have been preparing to rob the tollhouse, but had been put off my several passersby making their way home from a nearby dance.

In the meantime, John Miller's body was removed to his sister's house for mourning, and from there he was interred in the churchyard at Braco on the Saturday following his murder.

As was usual for any crime committed in rural Scotland during the Victorian era, any passing tramp, gypsy or navvy would immediately fall under suspicion. Two navvies found in a lodging-house at Crieff were arrested, then released when they could not be connected to the murder. In similar fashion, a tramp who had been spotted heading along the Comrie Road, in the direction of the Callander and Oban Railway Works was tracked down and arrested. He too was unconnected to the killing.

Nevertheless, despite these false leads, the net was beginning to close. A police constable in Alloa recognised the description of the clothes worn by the killer. He recalled that a tramp wearing those exact same garments had recently spent ten days in the local jail there for 'theft and disorderly conduct.' The man was George Chalmers (although he also employed the alias James Wilson). A description of Chalmers was issued:

'George Chalmers, alias James Wilson. Released from Alloa on December 20th, 1869. A native of Aberdeenshire, known to carry out casual farmwork. Ginger beard; red cheeks; has a stammer and walks with a stoop. Known for falling foul of the law.'

In an early example of an arrest 'mugshot', the police even circulated a glass plate photograph – with the rosy, red cheeks and ginger beard handily coloured in by officers.

In a further development, an Irish navvy was arrested by the Linlithgow Constabulary at Uphill, near Bathgate, on 5 January 1870. He gave his name as Owen McGechan. Although he was rumoured to have been in possession of clothing similar to that stolen from John Miller, and had probably been in the Dunblane area around the time of the murder, he was ultimately released. Although a highly suspicious character – he used a number of aliases – McGechan appeared to be younger than the description of the man released from Alloa Jail and therefore dismissed as a suspect. He was also married with two children, and had been living in Dundee, a factor which appeared to play in his favour. Following his release, McGechan disappeared without a trace. Three months later, he became a strong suspect in the horrific murder of a young girl in Stockwell Street, Glasgow. Unfortunately, he was never apprehended nor seen again.

A further six weeks passed, during which time seven arrests were made in Scotland and 40 in England, none of which turned out to be George Chalmers. It was feared that he may have escaped on a whaling boat, as he had once worked as a sea-whaler. A watch was put on several ports in Scotland

and the north of England, but to no avail. Eventually, public impatience led the Perthshire authorities to announce a reward of £50 (equivalent to £3,000 today) for information leading to an arrest. A billposter featuring a more detailed description was widely displayed in newspapers, post offices, police stations, and on billboards:

'FIFTY POUNDS REWARD
George Chalmers alias James Wilson
Labourer or Puddler, or Vagrant. Supposed native of Aberdeenshire. Age, about forty years. Height, 5 feet 4½ inches; Hair brown or reddish; Whiskers, reddish – short and thin round chin; Face shaved far back; no moustache; Low forehead, thick eyebrows; Eyes, hazel or grey – sunk in head; Nose, common, sharp, and slightly turned up at point; Complexion, fresh and ruddy; Face, longish, with high cheek bones and sharp pointed chin; Upper lip thick and turned up; front teeth of upper jaw visible, and one or two of them awanting; Make – stoutish, broad shoulders, long body and short legs; Weight 130 lbs; Marks – hollow on one side of his mouth, as if from want of teeth or part of jaw; Stutters or has a halt in his speech. He may be dressed in part of the stolen clothes.'

[A 'puddler' was a labourer who specialised in converting pig-iron into wrought iron.]

It was a melodramatic – verging on pantomime-esque – description, guaranteed to strike fear into the heart of every law-abiding, middle class newspaper reader. If ever a man's guilt could be predetermined by the prejudices of the Victorian criminal justice system, that man was George Chalmers.

Nevertheless, it would be a further three months until the wanted fugitive was finally apprehended.

On the morning of Saturday, 14 May, on the Arbroath Road, heading north from Dundee, Police Constable Billington finally arrested George Chalmers. Now five months since John Miller's murder the wanted man appeared to have relaxed his demeanour somewhat, making no effort to hide or avoid public places. Constable Billington had first observed his suspect in Dundee's Princes Street, during the early hours of the previous morning. The man's scruffy appearance (which Billington noted as 'bareheaded, without a coat, and having a ragged shirt') aroused the constable's interest and he engaged Chalmers in conversation. The wanted man explained to Billington that he was heading for Aberdeen, via Arbroath. The two men chatted for a few minutes, then Chalmers left, making his way towards the Arbroath High Road.

Constable Billington returned to Dundee Police Station just before 6am, to finish his shift, and mentioned the incident to the sergeant on duty. Immediately, the sergeant became convinced that the man matched the description of the individual wanted for the murder of John Miller in Braco, and the two policemen set off in pursuit of Chalmers, who by now had several hours head start. After an hour's fruitless searching, the two officers had only reached the Eastern Necropolis Cemetery. Billington was sent home to rest, following his long shift. However, the constable was desperate to catch the fugitive. He quickly changed his clothes and returned to join the search. By 8am he had reached Claypots Farm, four miles from Dundee, along the Arbroath Road. There in front of him, ambling nonchalantly, and making no effort to conceal himself, was the same man he had encountered in Princes Street approximately eight hours earlier. This time was carrying a potato sack over his shoulders.

Constable Billington at once informed the man, 'I am arresting you on suspicion of being George Chalmers, the person wanted and accused of the murder at Braco.'

Chalmers reacted with an air of innocence and indignation, replying, 'I know nothing of that. My name is Andrew Brown.'

Still smarting from the dressing down he had no doubt received as a result of failing to identify Chalmers in Princes

Street, Constable Billington arrested his suspect and escorted Chalmers to Broughty Ferry Police Station, where he was compared with the likeness of the man wanted for John Miller's murder. Despite claiming to be 'Andrew Brown', Chalmers' description matched that of the wanted man perfectly. He was then removed to Dundee Police Station to be interrogated by Inspector Stewart, who had arrived from Crieff following news of the arrest.

When asked by the Inspector to admit his real name, and reveal where he had been in December last year, Chalmers stated:

'My name is Andrew Brown. I am a hawker, but I occasionally sing on the streets.'

Nevertheless, the inspector was so convinced that the man was lying, Chalmers was charged on the spot for the murder of Miller – despite the absence of any real physical evidence. Chalmers shook his head and stated:

'Na, na, there's been a few taken up for that already; you'll need to let me awa' also.'

Under questioning Chalmers acknowledged that he had been jailed once in Wales, but he strenuously denied ever having been in prison anywhere else. He was asked directly if he had ever been incarcerated at Alloa Jail; an accusation he also refuted. Not to be dissuaded Inspector Stewart continued his interrogation:

'We know you've been there. So, there's no point you claiming otherwise.'

Eventually Chalmers buckled under pressure, admitting:

'There's no use me denying the thing any longer, my name is George Chalmers. I was liberated from Alloa Prison on the 20th December. After being freed, I went to Edinburgh, where I stayed till after the New Year; from Edinburgh I went to Glasgow; and from Glasgow I went to England. And that's the truth of it.'

Under further questioning, Chalmers continued to detail his movements:

'I moved about for two or three months this year. I again returned to Glasgow, and travelled from Glasgow to Stirling, and across Perthshire by Sheriffmuir. I reached Dundee on Friday night; and on Saturday morning I set out for Aberdeen.'

He emphatically denied any part in the tollkeeper's murder, and stated, 'I was not near that spot on the 21st December.'

Despite his continuing claims of innocence, Chalmers was kept in custody until Monday morning, before being escorted to Dunblane Jail. He was then indicted by Sheriff Grahame to stand trial for John Miller's murder, at the Perth Circuit Court of Justiciary on Tuesday, 6 September 1870.

21 - THE BRACO MURDER
(Part Two - The Trial)

Tuesday, 6 September 1870 – the day of Chalmers' trial, finally arrived. It is almost certain that the accused man was doomed before his ordeal had even begun.

In the months since his arrest, Chalmers had been interrogated at length by the police and coaxed into making two conflicting statements. These were dictated by Chalmers and transcribed, as it is doubtful he was able to read or write. Chalmers was then paraded around the streets of Braco, Crieff and Comrie in a bizarre form of public identification parade, in the hope that someone might recognise him. In addition, he was also questioned over the brutal murder of a young girl in Stockwell Street, Glasgow (mentioned in the previous chapter). This was duly reported in several newspapers – without restriction – a circumstance hardly likely to ensure him a fair trial.

However, these matters did not interest the public who had gathered in Perth to witness the eagerly awaited trial. The Lord Justice-Clerk and Lord Cowan occupied the bench. Mr Alexander Asher (who would later become Solicitor General for Scotland) conducted the prosecution for the Crown. Chalmers was defended by Andrew J Young, from Albany Street Chambers in Edinburgh.

The courtroom was ordered to be silent as the charge was read to the prisoner:

'On the 21st or 22nd December, 1869, in the house at Blackhill tollbar, in the parish of Ardoch, you, the prisoner, George Chalmers, attacked the tollkeeper, John Miller, with an iron crowbar or some other instrument, and struck him one or more blows on or near the head, and dashed his head violently against the floor, in consequence of which he died, and was thus murdered by you. How do you plead?'

Chalmers, who appeared unconcerned and had entered the dock smiling, sat down and did not stand when instructed. Positively bristling with irritation, Lord Cowan snapped at the accused man:

'Prisoner at the bar, stand up! This is a matter of murder!'

Chalmers rose to his feet and Lord Cowan addressed him again:

'Prisoner, are you guilty or not guilty or the crime of murder with which you stand charged?'

'No sir; I am not.' he replied defiantly.

However, before the Crown could begin the prosecution's case, Andrew Young QC approached the bench and requested the opportunity to enter a special defence plea on behalf of his client:

'Your honours, the defendant pleads generally not guilty, and especially at the time the crime was said to have been committed, he was not at Blackhill tollbar, but at Easter Manuel, in the parish of Muiravonside, in the shire of Stirling.'

The first witnesses to be called, Peter McLeish, Archibald McLaren and Mary Bayne, described the gruesome facts surrounding the discovery of John Miller's body.

'I did not touch the body,' Archibald McLaren explained, 'Miller was lying on his back, and his stick was near his left hand. The weather was frosty and the blood was dry. I saw some bread and cheese lying about the room.'

Archibald McLaren, who lived approximately half a mile away, also claimed to have seen George Chalmers one month earlier, between the bridge at Braco and Muthill. Before being dismissed he was shown several items of evidence and asked to identify them:

'I never saw that pocket-mirror you have just showed me in Miller's house before. He used to mend his bedclothes, and he had bits of cloth in the house. He did have a suit, though, like the piece of cloth you showed me.'

The next witness, Mary Bayne, then spoke:

'My impression, from the position of my brother's body,

was that he had got up from the chair and was defending himself when he fell. My brother kept his best clothes, tweeds, and shirts in the chest. I noticed that they were amissing. He kept his money in the chest where his clothes were. We didn't find the key to the chest till about Whitsunday though. It was in the fireplace. I think the man who committed this murder must have been oftener than once to my brother's place.'

Thomas Bayne (John Miller's cousin, who later found the key to the tollhouse in the dung heap), testified to seeing a coin-purse in Blackhill tollhouse:

'I remember seeing a purse of my cousin's, in which he kept some coins, usually two-penny bits and the like. And a handkerchief too.'

The witness was then asked if he recognised the items of evidence recovered from among George Chalmers' belongings.

'The handkerchief you showed me,' Thomas Bayne answered, 'is like the one my cousin used. But I can't say the purse belonged to him. I don't remember it having nicks in it. His handkerchief was of a similar pattern.'

In his cross-examination for the defence, Andrew Young QC attempted to discover more about the other man seen lurking in the street on the day before his murder.

'Mr Bayne, do you know who this man was?'

'No, sir, I did not know the man, but my cousin said that the man had been in his house between eleven and twelve on Monday night, and that they smoked a pipe together. He said the man was a new game-watcher, and that he stayed at Braco.'

'So, Mr Miller seemingly had no apprehension about this man, by the way he spoke of him?'

'No, sir.'

Superintendent of Police Peter Stewart was next to be called to the stand. He described the crime scene that greeted him:

'I saw Mr Miller's stick lying by his side and observed what I thought was blood and hair on the crowbar. I also examined the chests, one of which was locked. I burst it open. It appeared to have been ransacked, and I only found a penny in it. Then, on the 29th December, I searched through the discarded garments left behind by the murderer, and found a pawn ticket, some needles, a small tooth comb, some hair and gut, and two broken fishing hooks. In the pockets of a coat, which had been concealed behind the firewood, I found a watch key, a bone button, a pipe head, a vest, and a hair pin. When the prisoner was apprehended in Dundee, on him was found a handkerchief, a purse, a piece of cloth, and a pocket mirror. A pocket mirror had been on the mantelpiece of the deceased, according to the relatives, but it was no longer there when I searched the house.'

In cross-examination for the defence, and showing a remarkable foresight for the forensic preservation of a crime scene (something which was sadly lacking in the Victorian era), Young expressed some concern over the length of the time between the discovery of the body and the thorough search of the tollhouse. Superintendent Stewart replied, 'I did not make a thorough search on the 22nd as there was no time; but I made a hurried one. I left at three o'clock. It did not occur to me to search inside the clothes until the 29th.'

'So the back room at the tollhouse was not sealed at any time?'

'No. It was left in charge of the relatives.'

'So the house was not supervised?'

'The door of the house was sealed on the 22nd, and Constable Morgan remained on duty there.'

Constable Morgan was then called to the stand and asked to clarify the thoroughness of his watch over the property, 'I was summoned, and asked to maintain a watch of the tollhouse until Superintendent Stewart returned on the 23rd.'

'And on the 23rd, constable, was everything in the same place it had been the day before?'

'I do not know, sir. I was not actually present when the house was first searched on the 22nd.'

'Then how are you able to tell?'

'I sat in the back room on part of the night of the 23rd then patrolled in front of the house. As far as I saw, nobody had interfered with the house.'

'Very well, thank you, constable. No further questions.'

John Jack, a labourer from Braco, had been asked to take care of the tollhouse once the police had finished their investigations at the premises. He confirmed that 'the house was sealed up and the window nailed down.'

Mary Bayne, who perhaps knew the victim better than anyone else, testified next. While she able to confirm that several items were missing from the tollhouse, she added, 'The clothes you showed me did not belong to my brother. I never saw a pocket-mirror in his possession. I have seen a handkerchief like that one, but I can't identify the purse.'

Sergeant Samuel Ferguson, from Alloa Police Constabulary, confirmed that George Chalmers was indeed the same man he had arrested and jailed in Alloa on 10th December:

'He was tried and convicted for disorderly conduct, and sentenced to ten days' imprisonment. I found upon his person an awl, a pair of scissors, a pipe, a pawn ticket, watch key, fish hooks, toothcomb, and some hair. The vest and trousers that you now show me resemble the pair he had on at Alloa.'

'This seems like a lot of things, Sergeant?' observed Mr Asher.

'Prisoners generally have lots of things in their pockets, your honour.'

The fact that Chalmers already had a large number of items in his possession at least two weeks *before* John Miller's murder, did not aid the prosecution's case, however. It would now be almost impossible to confirm which, if any, of these items matched similar ones stolen from the tollhouse. The Crown's case also suffered a setback when Sergeant Ferguson confessed that 'the reward offered for the apprehension of George Chalmers assisted my recollection of the items, sir.'

A roar of laughter erupted in the public gallery and Mr Asher was forced to enquire, 'Have you then given us different evidence on account of that reward being offered?'

'No, sir. I never claimed or expected the reward, and I have spoken the truth.'

A string of witnesses followed, all of whom recognised Chalmers from the Falkirk Feeing Fair, and various lodging houses in Dunblane, Stirling and Crieff. Crucially for the Crown, Margaret Powers and Sarah Morrison both confirmed spotting Chalmers walking the streets around Braco and Muthill at Christmas and New Year. Sarah Morrison recalled buying a black surtout coat from Chalmers, although on examintion this appeared to be a month before John Miller's death.

John Nixon, a hawker from Dundee, gave evidence that 'The prisoner was in my house and left an old pocket handkerchief, a purse, and some pieces of cloth. Though, when I asked him about them, he said he had made the purse himself and that the handkerchief was his own.'

Next, the respected surgeon from Stirling, Dr William Hutton Forrest, gave details of the post-mortem. Dr Forrest, who was largely responsible for the introduction of a fresh-water supply to the area following one of the many cholera epidemics of the Victorian era, added much credibility to the prosecution's case:

'I was asked by the Procurator-Fiscal to go to Blackhill tollhouse and examine the deceased. The body was in an excellent condition, and free from putrefaction. The fingers were contracted. There was an incised wound made by an instrument having a blunt edge, three inches in length, and under this wound a bone was fractured and depressed. There was a similar wound in the right temple bone, two inches in length. There was a third wound of a similar character three inches in length, situated on the back part of the head, and the bone under it was also fractured and depressed. In addition to an incised wound on the right side of the nose, the head and face were soaked with blood, and the pool of blood on the floor was enormous, forming a parallelogram in shape, three feet by two.

The conclusion of my report is that the death of John Miller was caused by the application of external violence on the right side of the head. The violence was applied with much force, and the deceased must have lived for some time after the infliction of the violence, as demonstrated by the enormous escape of blood.'

'Thank you, Doctor, and is this sort the instrument which would inflict the wounds you saw?' enquired Mr Asher, dramitically brandishing the crowbar.

'Yes,' replied Dr Forrest, 'I believe he received at least three distinct blows. He could not have recovered from the blows received.'

The final evidence provided by the prosecution was two sworn statements given by the accused man to John Grahame, the Sheriff-Substitute of Perthshire, during his time in incarceration awaiting trial:

'I did not assault or murder John Miller. I never was at the village of Braco. I had no handkerchief or cloth like the one shown to me. The boots I was wearing, I begged from a man in Edinburgh.'

George Chalmers later added to his statement, claiming that on 21st and 22nd December:

'I went eight miles on the other side of Falkirk and got lodging in a farmhouse. I saw the farmer and spoke to him. He was an oldish man. The farmer put me in the cornhouse and I was locked in. It was about six in the evening. I was not let out till between seven and eight in the morning. I got some breakfast then I went to Edinburgh and on that night (22nd) I went to the Night Asylum. On the road, I met a man called Kenny and we picked up a woodcock, which we sold for sixpence, which we spent on hard ale. After two nights I went to Falkirk, then south by the Carron Iron Works to Edinburgh, and then to Berwick.'

The prosecution clearly felt there was little credibilty in the accused man's statements, as they were not submitted into evidence. It was now time for the defence to present their case to the jury.

As was usual in the majority of Victorian trials, the case for the defence was far briefer than that presented by the prosecution. With defendants not permitted to speak in their own defence in court until the 1880s capacity of the advocate to mount any sort of satisfactory defence relied heavily on being able to produce reliable, trustworthy and sympathetic witnesses. The obstacles in overcoming the prejudices of an all male, middle-class Victorian jury, who largely believed in the existence of the 'Criminal Class' and the inate respectabilty of all those in positions of authority, were almost insurmountable. Not only would these witnesses need to provide the accused man with a steadfast character reference and alibi, they would be required to overcome the inherent biases existing in nineteeth-century society.

James Horn, William Taylor, Margaret Gardiner, Peter Forgie and Alexander Taylor, all recalled Chalmers sleeping in the byre at Easter Manuel Farm regularly over December 1869 but, unfortunately for the defendant, could not recall the exact day – although they did remember him staying on a frosty night towards the end of the month (which it was on the night of the murder).

The defence's final witness, Mrs Pringle, failed to attend court, resulting in Police Constable William Morgan being despatched to Crieff to locate her. Unfortunately she had absconded from her lodging without paying her rent. It was the final nail in the defence's already thin case. Chalmer's advocate had only one option in his final summation to the jury – to plead for his client's life:

'Gentlemen of the jury, the one thought that must be uppermost in your minds now, is that you are engaged in an enquiry of the most serious and momentous nature. The life of a human being is dependent upon the judgment formed by this jury; and when such an issue is concerned, you cannot exercise too much caution in receiving what I am compelled to call the doubtful evidence which had been led by the Crown. You are in a delicate position, but you are bound to give a verdict in accordance with justice but, far more immediately, you are required *not* to fall into the awful and irretrievable error of condemning an innocent man.'

Lord Cowan summed up the evidence at length, reminding the jury of the 'serious and momentous nature of the proceedings.' His final comments were perhaps decisive in deciding the outcome of the trial:

'If you are of the opinion that the prisoner was at Braco on the night of 21st December, and that the clothing found in the tollhouse belongs to him, the fact that there were no eyewitnesses does not prevent you from returning a verdict according to your consciences. The prisoner ought to get the benefit of any reasonable doubt you may have; but, if you have no reasonable doubt, then your duty is to convict him.'

The jury retired at 2.20pm and returned at 3.20pm – exactly one hour later. Mr Jameson, the foreman, annouced:

'The jury, by a majority, find the prisoner guilty as libelled.'

'By what majority?'

'Thirteen to two.'

The Lord Justice-Clerk then addresseed the prisoner:

'George Chalmers, after a most patient healing, the jury has found you guilty of this most atrocious crime. I need not tell you that the verdict leaves me only one duty to discharge – that is, to pronounce upon you the last penalty of the law. I advise you to give the short time which the law now gives you – but, short as it is, it is much longer than that which your victim was allowed – in preparing for the fate which must inevitably overtake you. The sentence of the Court is follows – that you be removed from the bar to the county prison, there to be kept and fed on bread and water until the 4th October; and that day, between the hours of eight and ten in the morning, be executed within the walls of the prison. May God have mercy on your soul.'

Only as Lord Justice-Clerk's final words echoed around the courtroom, did those present finally notice any emotion on George Chalmers' face. He turned around and faced the rear of the dock before being led downstairs sobbing.

What next for the condemned man? There was immediate talk of an appeal. However, if that appeal failed, a recent change in the law would ensure that George Chalmers' planned execution was to be a historic and unique one.

22 - THE BRACO MURDER
(Part Three - The Execution)

Before considering the matter of Chalmers' appeal against his conviction and sentence, it is first important to address two questions: Was George Chalmers guilty, and did he receive a fair trial?

The answer to the first question is – possibly. He was an unsavoury character, prone to heavy drinking and had undoubtedly been guilty of several petty crimes during his short life, not least theft, drunkenness and disorderly behaviour. However, he had never been convicted for any offence involving serious violence. The standard of evidence required to achieve a guilty verdict in a murder trial (particularly one in which the penalty is hanging), is 'beyond all reasonable doubt.' Did the Crown really succeed in establishing that, in the case of George Chalmers?

Secondly, did he receive a fair trial? The answer to that question is almost certainly not. Remember, the job of the defence is only to establish some doubt in the defendant's guilt. If that is accomplished, then a jury should not convict. The two pillars on which the prosecution's case rested were:

1. That the items found in Chalmers' possession belonged to the victim, *or* identified him as the man who spent ten days in Alloa Prison two weeks prior to John Miller's murder (thus proving that Chalmers was within twenty miles of Braco two weeks prior to the murder – hardly proof of murder). 2. That the man seen in the vicinity of Braco on or around the date of the murder must be the same person who killed John Miller. Yet, there is no definite proof that this person is linked to the murder. Firstly, several of the witnesses failed to, or were unsure if, the clothing stolen from the tollhouse was the same clothing found in Chalmers' possession at the time of his arrest. Secondly, there seems to be conflicting evidence

concerning the provenance of at least some of the items found in his pockets when apprehended (such as the pocket mirror). At least some of these objects already appear to have been owned by Chalmers, and were logged in the prison ledger at Alloa two weeks *before* John Miller's death, and therefore, cannot have belonged to the murdered man.

Despite these serious discrepancies, perhaps the biggest flaw in Chalmers' conviction is the Crown's supposition that the stranger seen in the vicinity in the days prior to the murder, *must* therefore be the killer. No definite proof links this hypothesis; it is a supposition at best. Yet, the extensive police search, the description, the 'Wanted' poster, the reward and the public parading of George Chalmers along the streets of Braco and Dunblane, all points towards the conflation of two separate assumptions.

Chalmers' appointed solicitor, Andrew Paul from Dundee, certainly thought the conviction an unsafe one. He wrote to the Home Secretary and appealed for a commuting of the condemned man's sentence. His letter outlined the following concerns regarding the conviction:

'1st, The insufficiency of the evidence, which it character-ised as entirely circumstantial, and resting exclusively on coincidences ; 2nd, The open and unsuspicious behaviour of the prisoner immediately after the murder and before his apprehension; 3rd, The disadvantages accruing to the prisoner from the manner of collecting the evidence against him; 4th, On the confirmation of the prisoner's statement, that he was at the farmhouse near Linlithgow on the night of the murder; 5th, On the fact that the prosecution had nine months in which to collect their evidence, and in that time got ninety-seven witnesses, all of whom being quite unknown to Chalmers or his agent. Yet, all of whom needed to be questioned by the defence, before the nature of that defence could be decided on – and for which the prisoner had only twelve clear days, it being thus impossible either to see all the Crown witnesses for precognition, or to collect their evidence.

And lastly, on the calm and consistent conduct of the prisoner, from the time of his apprehension until now, and his strong assertions of innocence.'

The appeal, comprehensive as it was, failed to even mention the Crown's unfounded assumption that the man seen in the vicinity of the tollhouse must also be the murderer. Nor did the appeal mention the (at least) five other men who were arrested by the police on suspicion of the murder, questioned and subsequently released. Neither does the appeal mention the accused man's state of mind during the trial. His mental capacity was 'limited', according to the *Dundee Courier*, and his ability to fully understand the proceedings also seems to have been in doubt. In fact, the *Dundee Courier*'s court reporter commented on Chalmers' behaviour during the trial:

'During three fourths of the proceedings the prisoner lay forward with his head and hands on the railing of the bar, and when tired of this position he turned his head in the opposite direction and, with the same vacant stare, eyed the jury. When asked to stand up, so that the witnesses might look at him, he sprang to his feet with alacrity, and had no sooner resumed his seat, than he assumed his former attitude. He looked quite unconcernedly at the witnesses for the prosecution and at no part of the trial did he seem to follow the evidence for more than a minute or two.'

Chalmers' siblings also believed his mental capacity was limited due to 'problems with alcohol' exacerbated by 'sunstroke and brain fever.'

Meanwhile, Reverend McLaren of Fraserburgh took a keen interest in the doomed man, and garnered several hundred signatures on a petition for Chalmers' release, which was also forwarded to the Home Secretary. Reverend McLaren visited Chalmers in Perth Prison on several occasions, and was present when Sheriff Barclay informed the condemned man of the Home Secretary's response to the appeal. He noted the facts in his journal:

'Until afternoon between twelve and one o'clock, Chalmers

was in entire ignorance of the efforts which had been made on his behalf to obtain a commutation of his sentence. At that hour Sheriff Barclay, accompanied, by the Reverend Mr Clair (the prison chaplain), and a warder, entered his cell. The Sheriff informed him what had been done on his behalf, and stated that he had just received from the Home Secretary an answer to the petitions forwarded to him. He then read the letter, which in substance stated: "After communicating with the Judge who had presided at the trial, I have come to the conclusion that I see no reason for altering the sentence which has been passed, and that therefore the execution must take place on the day appointed."

While the Sheriff read the letter, Chalmers listened earnestly, but with an expression on his face which clearly showed that he did not understand the nature of the intelligence the Sheriff was communicating.'

Following the failure of his appeal, Chalmers spent his time in his cell glancing through a bible or deep in discussion with the prison chaplain. Something of his past was revealed in these conversations. Until the late 1850s, Chalmers had lived with his parents in pendicle accommodation at Fraserburgh. Unfortunately, following their deaths he was thrown out of the home, and forced into an itinerant life of destitution. He soon became addicted to drink, resulting in several arrests for disorderly behaviour, although he assured the prison chaplain:

'I have never been guilty of any inhumane act. Drunkenness was my greatest crime and, except for that, I have never been imprisoned. I have never robbed any man, nor have I stolen from any house. I am innocent of the murder of the poor old tollman near Braco, and after my death it is sure the true murderer will be discovered.'

Despite his protestations of innocence, the day of destiny soon dawned. Executions were a sadly common feature in nineteenth-century Britain, however, a recent change in the law would create additional public interest in Chalmers' hanging. His execution was to be the first non-public hanging to take place in Scotland, following the passing of the Capital Punishment (Amendment) Act 1868. Growing discontent among the establishment at the 'scandalous and revolting scenes' which often accompanied public executions had resulted in this amendment to the law.

Those members of the community who found the spectacle of a public hanging to be raucous (and cheap!) entertainment would now be catered for vicariously, by an incredibly detailed report of Chalmers' execution in the *Dundee Courier*, which although macabre and coldly matter of fact, nonetheless provides us with a fascinating insight into the final hours of a condemned man:

'Chalmers generally ate and slept well. His couch consisted of a straw mattress and blankets; but he was never allowed to retire to rest without first being handcuffed, and a warder placed beside him for the night.

The indispensable functionary at an execution (William Calcraft the hangman) arrived in Perth on Saturday aboard the mail train. He proceeded to the prison, where quarters had been provided for him. The privacy with which all executions are now effected has been marked in the present case. All the necessary preparations were completed almost without anyone knowing about them. Instead of the crowds of people, which, from a morbid curiosity, were led on previous similar occasions to gather and witness the erection of the scaffold, and spend the long dreary hours of the night till the hour when the condemned man was launched into eternity, there was an entire absence of persons on the streets.

On Sunday night the prisoner slept very little and appeared somewhat restless.

On Monday 2nd October, Chalmers was visited in the morning, afternoon, and evening by the Chaplain, who spent a considerable time with Chalmers in earnest prayer.

Perhaps the most distressing scene to be witnessed in the unfortunate man's cell was a visit from his two brothers James and William Chalmers, and his brother-in law, William Macdonald. When the men met each other face to face not one syllable was any of them able to utter for some time, all having burst into tears. The scene was painful to witness.

On Monday night he retired to rest about ten o clock. But again, sleep was denied to his eyelids, and he passed another sleepless night. At six o'clock a warder entered Chalmers' cell with his breakfast, which consisted of tea and bread. After breakfasting the chaplain commenced devotional exercises.

The Reverend gentleman, however, was latterly obliged to confess with sorrow that he was disappointed with the condemned man's frame of mind. As his last hour approached, he seemed to have become more callous and indifferent than penitent. He affirmed again and again that he was innocent.

On Tuesday morning, Lord Provost Pullar and other dignitaries assembled in Perth, and after all had formed in procession, they marched to the prison, preceded by the town's officers, attired in scarlet uniforms. Precisely at half-past seven the prison gate was opened, and the procession admitted. The gate having been again closed, all stood in the courtyard immediately in front of the prison office. Also present were Mr Welch, Superintendent of Police, Mr Wilson, the Governor of the jail, the press, and four police officers. Sheriff Barclay handed the death-warrant to the Lord Provost, and it was read aloud. This having been done the small company was conducted through a long corridor, to the cell of the condemned man. A table, on which a number of Bibles were placed, was set in the middle of the corridor. The Reverend Fleming stood facing Chalmers' open cell door. Bibles having then been distributed among the group, the Reverend Mr Fleming read the 1st, 2nd, 3rd, 4th, 12th, 13th, and 14th verses of the 8th Psalm. The chaplain then read the 51st Psalm, beginning with the words, "Have mercy upon me O God, according to thy loving kindness; according to the multitude of thy tender mercies blot out my transgressions."

The scene was solemn. A silence prevailed throughout the place, for the benefit of one who, in a few moments, would no longer be in the land of the living. The solemn voice of the clergyman, as he read from the Bible, was the only sound which broke upon the stillness. Meanwhile Chalmers leant against the side of the cell door, but appeared to be more listless than concerned. The Lord Provost stepped forward to the door of the cell, and addressed the prisoner:

'I have been asked by my brother Magistrates to ask if you have anything to convey to your friends, or any communication you wish to make?'

The Prisoner replied, 'I have nothing to say, but I would like this letter which I have written to be sent to my sister.'

'That is the only communication you have to make to your friends?'

'Yes,' replied the prisoner.

The Reverend Mr Fleming then said to the prisoner, 'I have just one word to say to you. It is my duty as a minister of the Gospel to say to you that a sin unconfessed is a sin unpardoned and a sin unforgiven, and those who are guilty expose themselves to an everlasting doom. If you go into the great eternity that is now before you with a lie upon your lips, we have reason to fear that you are upon the brink of everlasting ruin, and upon the very verge of the bottomless pit. I ask you, in the sight of God, to relieve us from the very distressing position in which we are placed by saying whether or not you are guilty of the awful crime for which you are condemned to suffer.'

Chalmers in a firm voice replied, 'I am innocent, sir; that is all I can say to you.'

The Lord Provost then introduced the prisoner to Calcraft, who carried with him his rope and binding straps. The prisoner wore the same outfit in which he had appeared at the trial. Having been offered a glass of wine, he lifted the glass and drank off its whole contents. He stood erect with the utmost composure in the centre of the cell, and quietly submitted to the executioner pinioning his arms. He even helped Calcraft to adjust one of the straps on his right wrist. Everything about Chalmers, in fact, showed that the prisoner had ceased to pay any attention to the appearance of the outer man. He neither wore cravat nor necktie, and his neck was greatly exposed. The pinioning having been completed, the Lord Provost and Magistrates proceeded to the prison yard, and stood about twenty feet from the scaffold. This hideous erection had been placed opposite the Governor's house, the platform being twenty feet from the ground.

The drop in the centre was surrounded by a railing between four and five feet high, on which was suspended a curtain of black cloth. Due to the floor of the drop being raised, the prisoner and the executioner are visible only from the head to the waist during the brief interval necessary for the ghastly toilette of death. Then the drop falls, and the condemned man entirely disappears, and the spectacle is at an end.

The chimes of eight o'clock of the bell of St John's Church had just died away when the prisoner, accompanied by the clergyman and Calcraft, emerged from the prison towards the courtyard. The prisoner walked unaided, and when within twelve feet of the wooden stair leading to the scaffold, he went off at a rapid pace, and almost ran up the steps to the drop. He was placed beneath the fatal beam and surveyed all around him as the clergyman and the executioner reached the bottom of the steps.

When Calcraft reached him, Chalmers looked into his face and smiled, and while the former was putting a noose on the rope, the wretched man intently watched the whole operation. Just as the rope was about to be placed round his neck, he waved his head from side to side and stretched out his neck, and while the executioner was adjusting the rope the doomed man said in a loud and clear voice,

'I know nothing of this affair. I will die like a man for it; yes, I will. But I was not there at all. I am innocent.'

While Calcraft was fastening the other end of the rope to the crossbeam, the Reverend Mr Fleming spoke to the condemned man,

'Jesus said, 1 am the resurrection and the life. The last enemy that shall be destroyed is death. Fear not, for 1 am with thee; be not dismayed, for 1 am thy God.'

The rope having been finally adjusted, the grey-bearded executioner drew from his pocket the hideous white cap, and pulled it over the head of the culprit, shutting out for ever from his sight everything pertaining to this world. The Reverend Mr Clair for the final time put the question to him whether he was guilty or innocent. To this Chalmers replied in loud and firm voice,

'May the Lord have mercy on me. Farewell for evermore. Thank God, I am innocent.'

The words had hardly escaped from his lips when the hangman grasped the hand of the victim as a last farewell, and with a sudden jerk the bolt was drawn, and the condemned man was launched into eternity. His body entirely disappeared from sight, and nothing could be seen from the ground save the rope by which he was suspended. He struggled but little, and then all was perfectly still. When the bolt was drawn a black flag was hoisted above the prison wall, and this was all by which the public could learn that the culprit had paid the penalty for his crime. There were not more than forty persons stood in the street adjoining the prison, who had gathered to see the flag hoisted.

After hanging the allotted time required by law, the body was cut down and interred in an unmarked grave within the prison walls.

Some of those present could only account for the extraordinary behaviour of the condemned man on the scaffold by the supposition that he must have been insane, or that he must have had hardened feelings beyond human comprehension.

Even Calcraft remarked that in all his experience he had never seen a man act with such bravado and firmness on the point of death.

It would be Perth Prison's final execution of the nineteenth century.

Lord Provost Pullar kept his word and passed on Chalmers' final letter to his sister in Peterhead:

'Perth Prison, 3rd October, 1870.
My Dear Sister,
l received both your letters. The first was read to me by the Governor; and the last one by Sheriff Barclay. And, Oh!, I felt very sad when listening to your kind and faithful words, while tears ran down my cheeks. I know they are the last letters I will get from you. I confess with sorrow that I have been a most wicked man for these last twelve years. I disobeyed all the good counsels of our dear father and mother. I left my home and took to a wandering life, which led me into evil company which I now most bitterly regret. My dear sister, strong drink has been my ruin and has been the cause of all my troubles. Oh that I had taken your many advices, and kept free that accursed drink; it has brought thousands of men and women to shame and misery, and so it has brought me. I now see the folly of

my ways, and what my reckless life has brought me.

My dear sister. I wish you would allow this letter to be made public after my death for the benefit of my fellow-creatures, that they may take warning from my sinful and profligate life, and its melancholy end.

So farewell, my dear sister, I remain your loving but unfortunate brother,

George Chalmers

Was Chalmers' final letter a confession of guilt for the murder of John Miller, or merely an expression of anguish at his wasted life? We will never know the truth.

TIPPERMUIR BOOKS

Tippermuir Books Ltd is an independent publishing company based in Perth, Scotland.

PUBLISHING HISTORY

The Piper of Tobruk: Pipe Major Robert Roy, MBE, DCM (2019)

The 'Gig Docter o Athole': Dr William Irvine & The Irvine Memorial Hospital (2019)

Afore the Highlands: The Jacobites in Perth, 1715–16 (2019)

'Where Sky and Summit Meet': Flight Over Perthshire – A History: Tales of Pilots, Airfields, Aeronautical Feats, & War (2019)

Diverted Traffic (2020)

Authentic Democracy: An Ethical Justification of Anarchism (2020)

'If Rivers Could Sing': A Scottish River Wildlife Journey. A Year in the Life of the River Devon as it flows through the Counties of Perthshire, Kinross-shire & Clackmannanshire (2020)

A Squatter o Bairnrhymes (2020)

In a Sma Room Songbook: From the Poems by William Soutar (2020)

The Nicht Afore Christmas: the much-loved yuletide tale in Scots (2020)

Ice Cold Blood (2021)

The Perth Riverside Nursery & Beyond: A Spirit of Enterprise and Improvement (2021)

Fatal Duty: Police Killers and Killer Cops: the Scottish Police Force 1812-1952 (2021)

The Shanter Legacy: The Search for the Grey Mare's Tail (2021)

'Dying to Live': The Story of Grant McIntyre, Covid's Sickest Patient (2021)

The Black Watch and the Great War (2021)

Beyond the Swelkie: A Collection of Poems & Writings to Mark the Centenary of George Mackay Brown (2021)

Sweet F.A. (2022)

A War of Two Halves (2022)

A Scottish Wildlife Odyssey (2022)

In the Shadow of Piper Alpha (2022)

Mind the Links: Golf Memories (2022)

Perthshire 101: A Poetic Gazetteer of the Big County (2022)

The Banes o the Turas: An Owersettin in Scots o the Poems bi Pino Mereu scrievit in Tribute tae Hamish Henderson (2022)

Walking the Antonine Wall: A Journey from East to West Scotland (2022)

The Japan Lights: On the Trail of the Scot Who Lit Up Japan's Coast (2022)

Fat Girl Best Friend: 'Claiming Our Space' – Plus Size Women in Film & Television (2023)

Wild Quest Britain: A Nature Journey of Discovery through England, Scotland & Wales – from Lizard Point to Dunnet Head (2023)

Guid Mornin! Guid Nicht! (2023)

Madainn Mhath! Oidhche Mhath! (2023)

Who's Aldo? (2023)

A History of Irish Republicanism in Dundee (c1840 to 1985) (Rùt Nic Foirbeis, 2024)

The Stone of Destiny & The Scots (John Hulbert, 2024)

The Mysterious Case of the Stone of Destiny: A Scottish Historical Detective Whodunnit! (David Maule, 2024)

Salvage (Mark Baillie, 2024)

Perthshire's Pound of Flesh (Mark Bridgeman, 2024)

A Most ~~Unsuitable~~ *Beautiful* Game: Celebrating Scottish Women's Football Fifty Years After the Ban (Karen Fraser, Julie McNeill & Fiona Skillen (editors), 2024)

FORTHCOMING

William Soutar: Collected Works, Volume 1 Published Poetry (1923– 1946) (Paul S Philippou (Editor-in-Chief) & Kirsteen McCue and Philippa Osmond-Williams (editors), 2024)

William Soutar: Collected Works, Volume 2 Published Poetry (1948– 2000) (Paul S Philippou (Editor-in-Chief) & Kirsteen McCue and Philippa Osmond-Williams (editors), 2024)

William Soutar: Collected Works, Volume 3 (Miscellaneous & Unpublished Poetry) (Paul S Philippou (Editor-in-Chief) & Kirsteen McCue and Philippa Osmond-Williams (editors), 2026)

William Soutar: Collected Works, Volumes 4-6 (Prose Selections) (Paul S Philippou (Editor-in-Chief) & Kirsteen McCue and Philippa Osmond-Williams (editors), 2027+)

The Black Watch From the Crimean War to the Egyptian Campaign (Derek Patrick and Fraser Brown (editors), 2024/5)

Drystone: A Gathering of Terminology and Technique (Nick Aitken, 2024)

The Lass and the Quine (Ashley Douglas (writer), Katie Osmond (illustrator), 2025)

The Royal Edinburgh Military Tattoo: 'The Show Must Go On' – Travels of the Tattoo Producer (Brigadier Sir Melville Jameson, 2024)

Balkan Rhapsody (Maria Kassimova-Moisset, translated from the Bulgarian by Iliyana Nedkova, edited by Cara Blacklock, 2024)

Button Bog And Other Voices & Treasures From A Traveller's Kist (Jess Smith, 2024)

A Wildlife Guide to Edinburgh (Keith Broomfield, 2024/5)

The Road to Mons Graupius (Alan Montgomery, 2024/5)

The Whole Damn Town (Hannah Ballantyne, 2025)

Blood Beneath Ben Nevis

£9.99

Mark Bridgeman

In *Blood Beneath Ben Nevis* Mark Bridgeman has created a fascinating collection of tales, events and folklore from around Lochaber, all focused around the uncanny, the disturbing, and the downright odd. Despite the mysterious overtones, the newspaper clippings on the back cover give the sense that what you are about to read happened to real people in a very real past. The landscape and the places are recognisable, as are the characters, with many of the familiar names living on in Lochaber today.

Perthshire's Pound of Flesh
£9.99

Mark Bridgeman

Perth, Blairgowrie, Crieff, Pitlochry, Aberfeldy all feature as well as the wider Perthshire area. Twenty-four true stories of murder, mystery and deception from around Perthshire. The secret of wartime SS prisoners held in Comrie is told, and the victims of witch-hunt trials are remembered. *Perthshire's Pound of Flesh* follows the success of *The River Runs Red* and *Blood Beneath Ben Nevis*, by the same author.